Artology: The Coloring Book; Apprentice Edition
(A Designs By Drew Collection)

Drew Calahan

Copyright © 2016 H.A. "Drew" Calahan

All rights reserved.

ISBN-13: 978-1987729108

DEDICATION

This collection is dedicated to every, friend, family, teacher , co-worker and stranger whom inspired me in some fashion to create the art you now hold in your hand.

A Message From the Artist:

What you hold in your hands is two decades worth of art. When I first set out to put this collection together, I had thought about having a theme, a "message" to the collection. Then it dawned on me, that the only message I really wanted to express was "Enjoy my art!" Not all of the pieces are pristine. Some are finer tuned than others; that is by design. This collection assembles an assortment of subject matters, with a flavor for nearly any person to enjoy. Unlike most other coloring books, I have included a table of contents. As you can see, the pieces are arranged alphabetically. That was how I choose to build this collection. Many pieces are in gray-tones, and may appear to be challenging to color over. DO IT! What fun is there in un challenging art? Feel free to allow my work, or your colors on my work to inspire you to make your own new creations. I would love to see what you do. Please send photos of your colored pages to *drew.5gstudios@gmail.com* I love being interactive with fans. Fan-art (color overs) will qualify for future give-a-ways.

About the variant editions:

Standard Edition: Basic coloring book, approximately 79 images.

Apprentice Edition: The basic 79 images plus an additional "complete your own" section of 20 partially complete images based on images in the Standard Edition.

Journeyman Edition: *RECCOMMENDED FOR MATURE AUDIENCES ONLY!!* Comes with the basic 79 images as well as 14 additional images of a more mature/graphic nature. Contains nudity and some violent elements.

Deluxe Edition: *RECCOMMENDED FOR MATURE AUDIENCES ONLY!!* This edition contains 113 images!!! All 79 basic coloring book images + all 20 complete your own images + all 14 Mature/graphic images.

Like any of the prints shown here-in? Visit **www.redbubble.com/people/geekyinker**

Order prints, t-shirts, wall décor, home décor and more. You can also see many pieces of work not shown in this collection. Be sure to check out:

www.redbubble.com/people/geekyinker/collections/856514-coloring-book-collection

for color your own options that go beyond the borders of a coloring book.

Table of Contents:

Agony	1
Art Teacher, The	3
Artist's Adoration, The	5
Balloon Race On a Hazy Day	7
Bird Jungle	9
Birth of an Amoeba, The	11
Both Sides	13
CloverFace	15
Connectivity	17
Contour 94'	19
Corridor	21
Cosmic Duelities	23
Cup Holder, The	25
Dear Deer	27
Departure	29
Downward I	31
Drake, the Daisy	33
Elements	35
Face First	37
Facelessness	39
Fairy's Ride, A	41
Fallen	43
Fallen Star	45
Filth and the Magic Sponge, The	47
Flamed	49
Foot Study	51
Hand Delivery	53
Hand Fishing	55
Hand Study	57
HandPrint	59
Help!	61
Here's Mud and a Dove In Your Eye	63
Homage to Stonehenge	65
Horrus, the Horse: Animal Study #1	67
Illusage #1	69
Illusage #2	71
Kiale, the Koala: Animal Study #2	73
Label Me Schooled	75
Lady and the Lily Pad, The	77
Lady and the Lily Pad, The (black /white)	79
Librarian, The	81
Lover's Lane I	83
Lover's Lane II	85
Lover's Lane III	87
Lover's Lane Complete	89
Man & Beast	91
Man on Fire	93
Masked Symmetry	95
Melted Still	97
Merlyn's Cave	99
MoonScape 1	101
MoonScape 2	103
MoonScape 3	105
MoonScape Complete	107
More Than Meets the Light	109
Nose Rose	111
Porcupine Cabin	113
Room With a View, A	115
Ruler of the Sky: Concrete Poem	117
Salted Sails	119
Scar, The	121
Shadows and Scratches	123
SkullRose	125
Snow Play	127
Society	129
Something Spocky This Way Comes	131
Sound of a Fossil, The	133
Still Conversation, A	135
Sun Fun Village	137
Timeout	139
Traveler's Exodus	141
Twin Balance View of Colorado, A	143
Wasteland	145
Whiskey Genie	147
White Tiger	149
WildFlower	151
World Wide Tiger	153

Apprentice Edition Bonus Content:
These selections are "complete your own" challenges.

6N1 Trace Design I	157
6N1 Trace Design II	159
Both Sides: Draft Parts	161
CloverFace: Pencil Sketch:	163
CloverFace: Conversion	165
Cosmic Duelites: Draft	167
Cup Holder, The: Stage I	169
Cup Holder, The: Stage II	171
Masked Symmetry Parts I & II	173
Mother's Eye	175
Orca Odyssey (Incomplete)	177
Palm Trees I	179
Palm Trees II	181
Poisoned Celestial	183
Snake Daisy: Stage I	185
Snake Daisy: Stage II	187
Snake Daisy: Stage III	189
WildFlower: Pencil Sketch	191
WildFlower: Construction	193

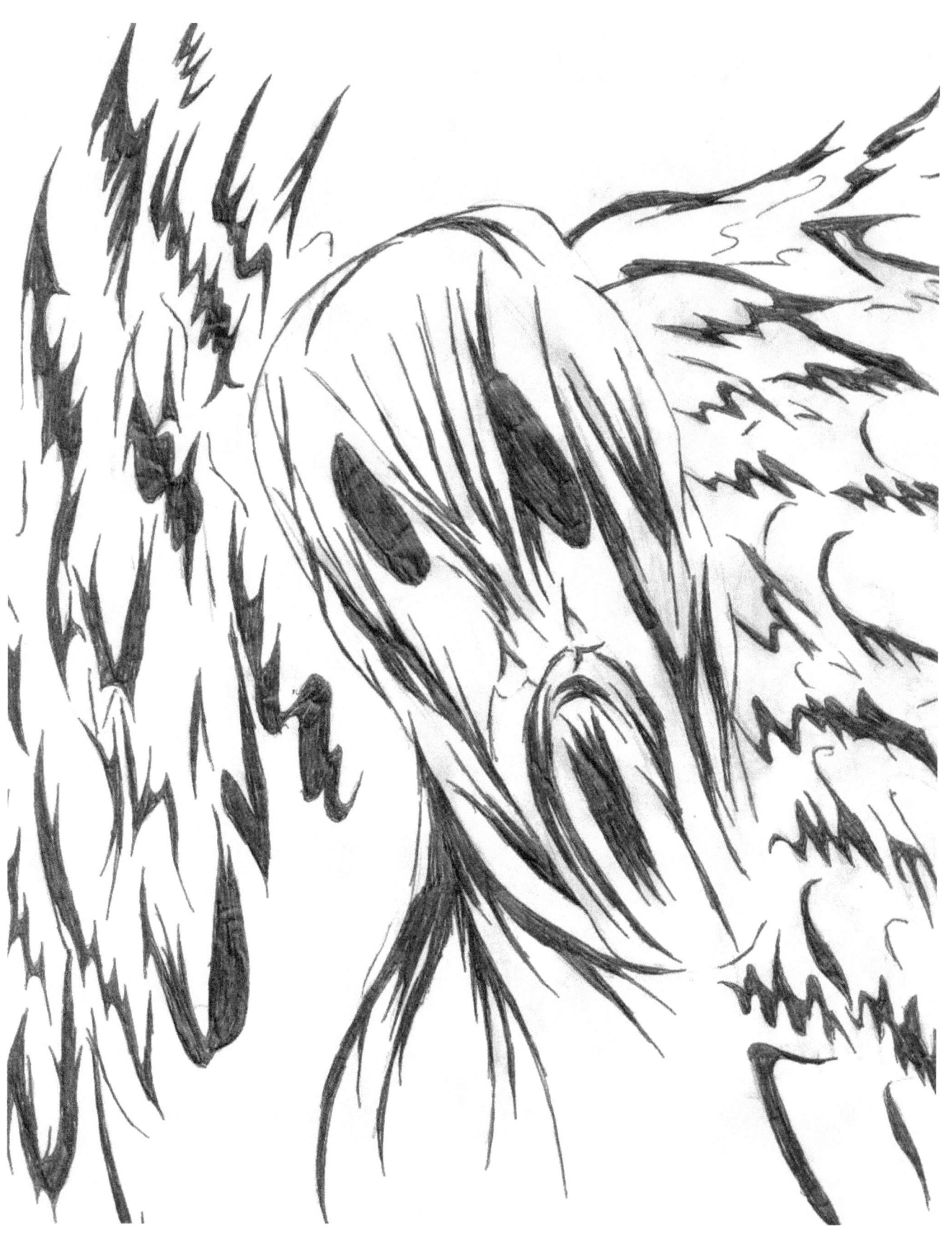

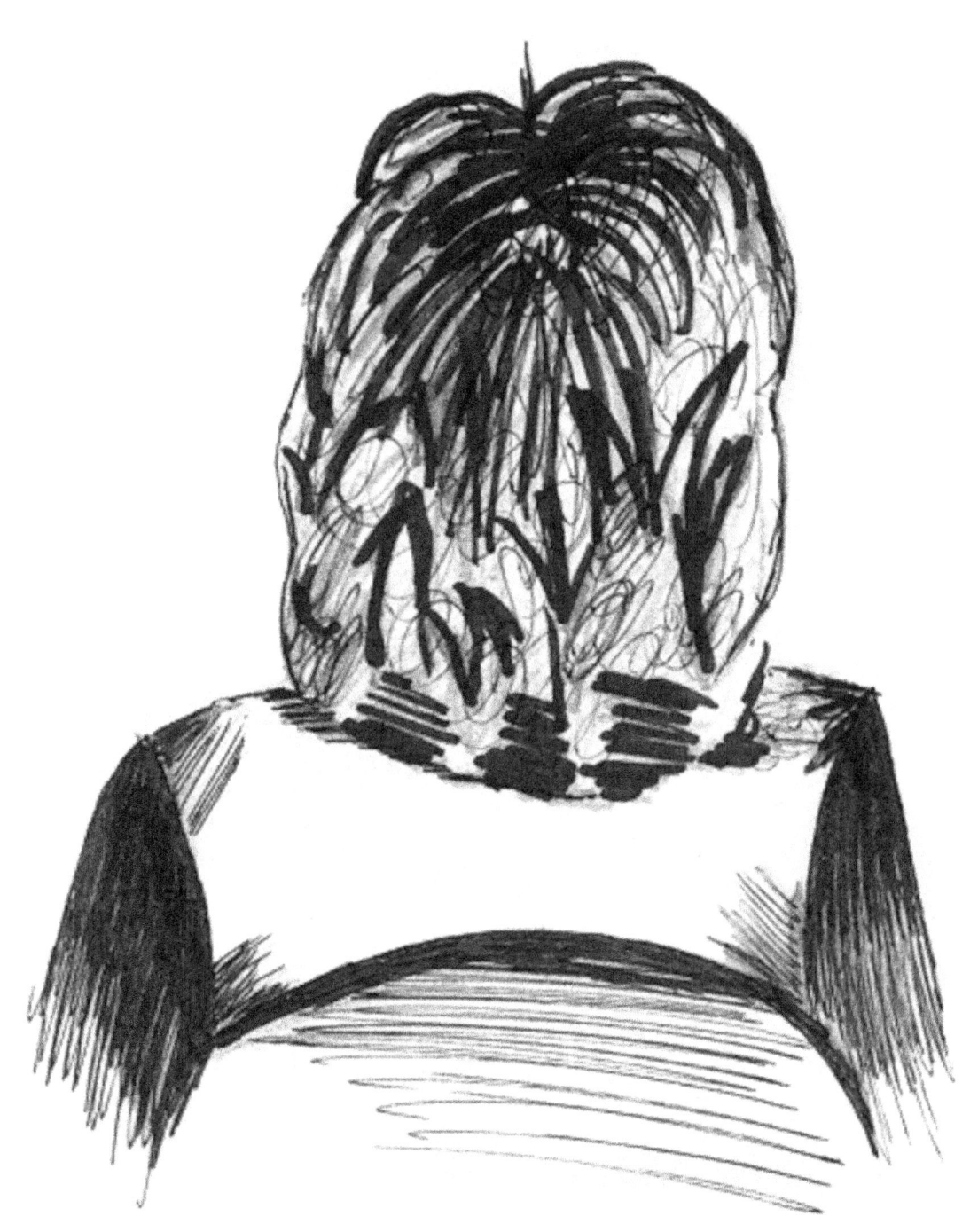

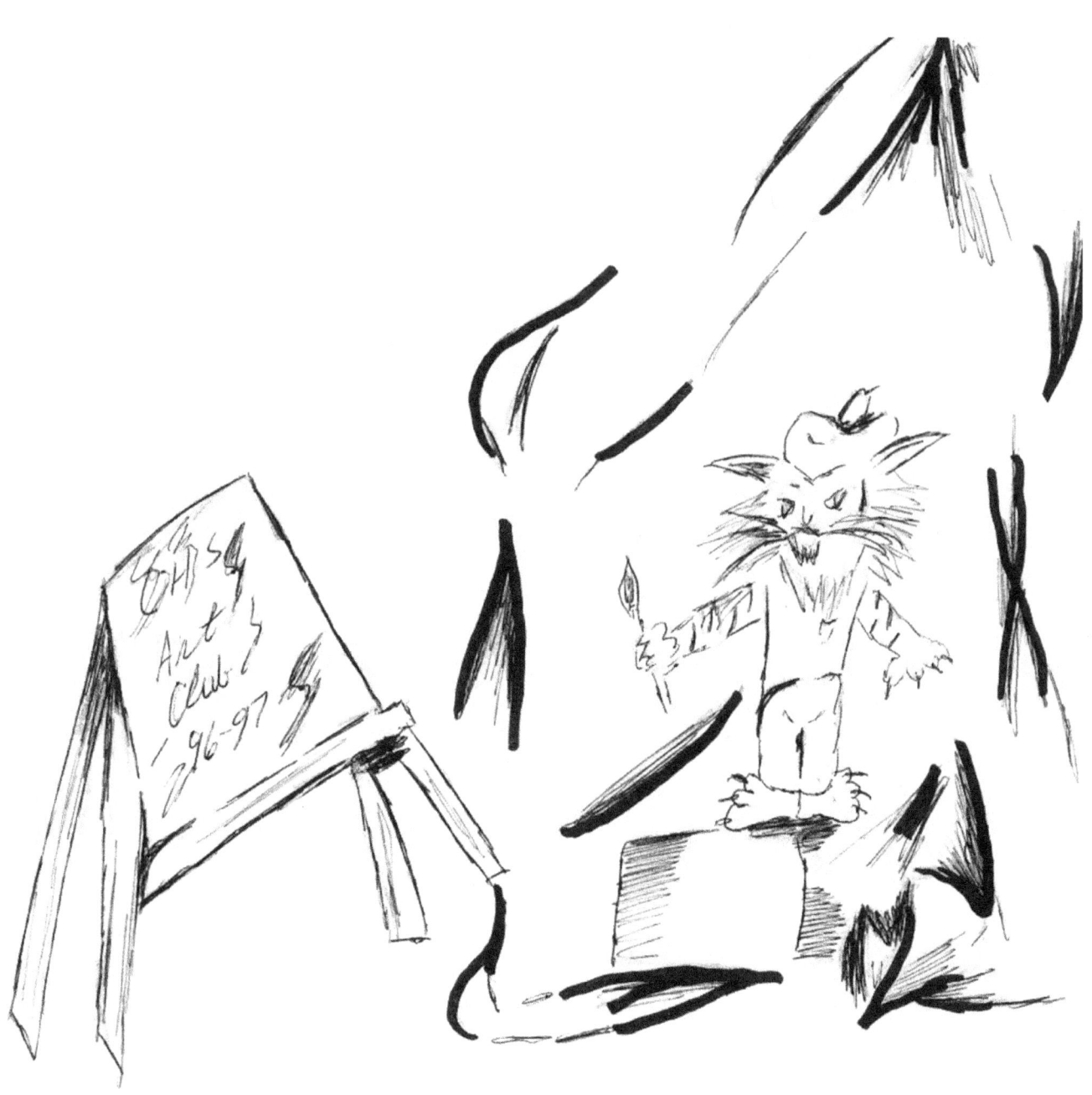

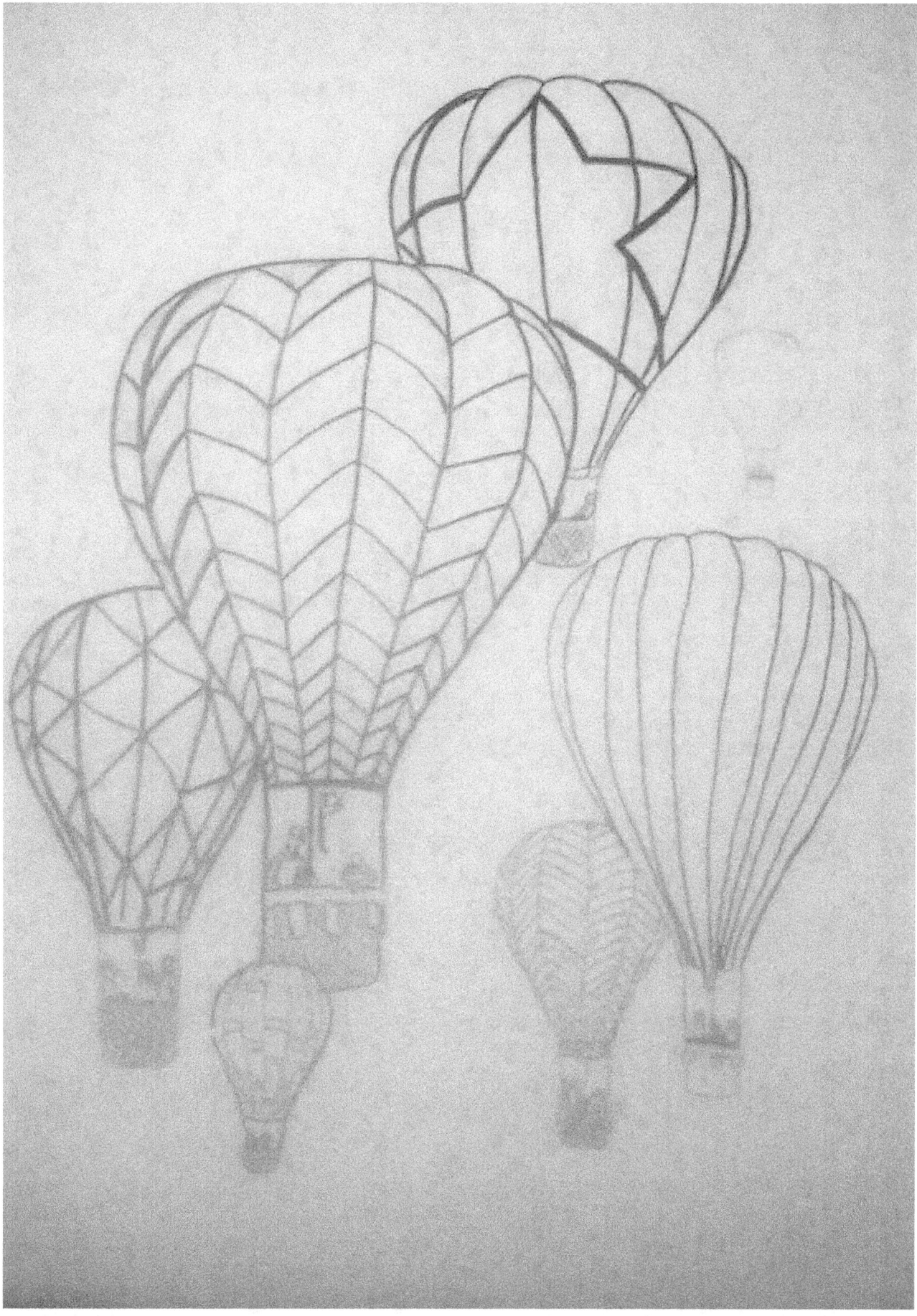

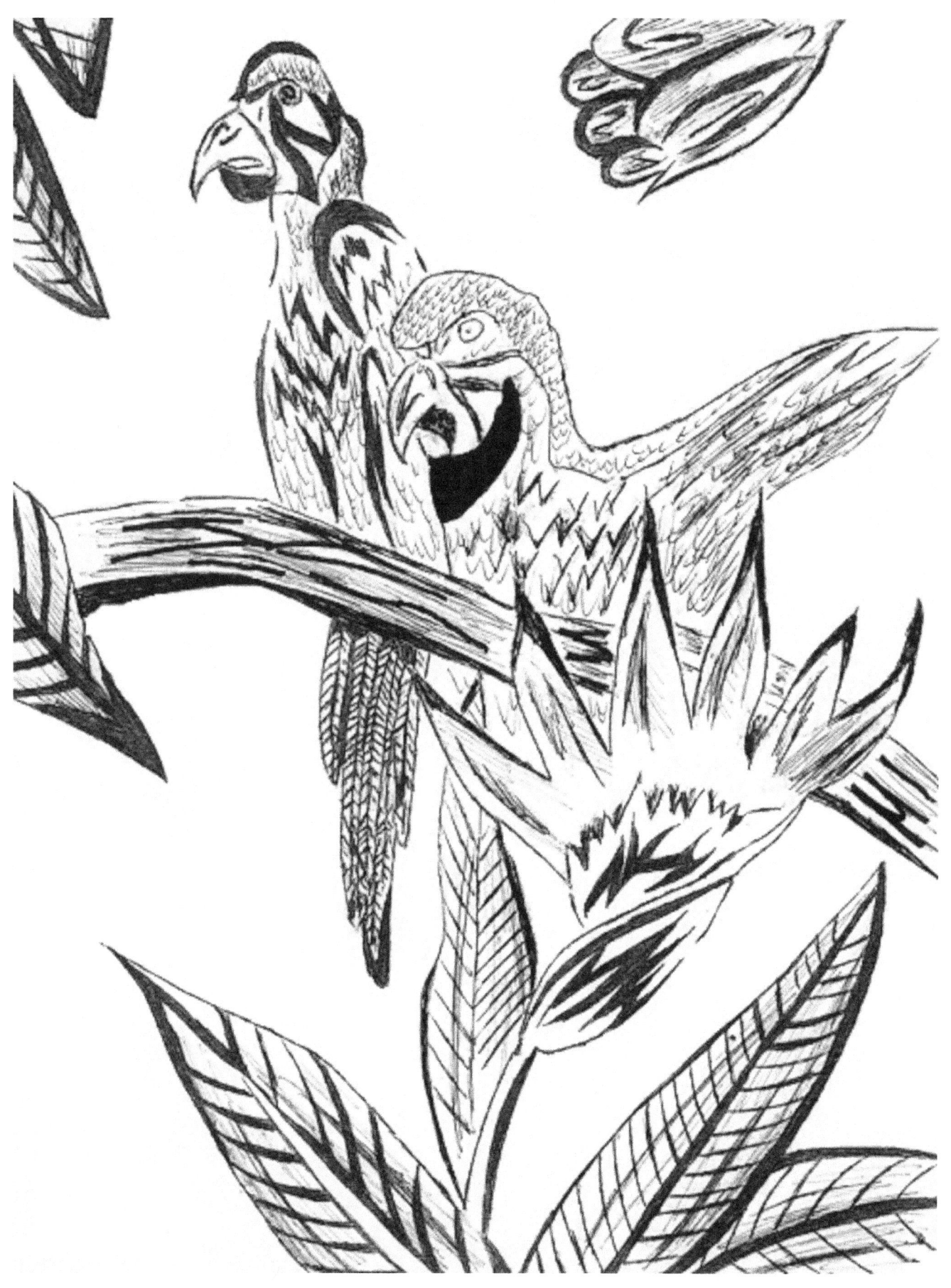

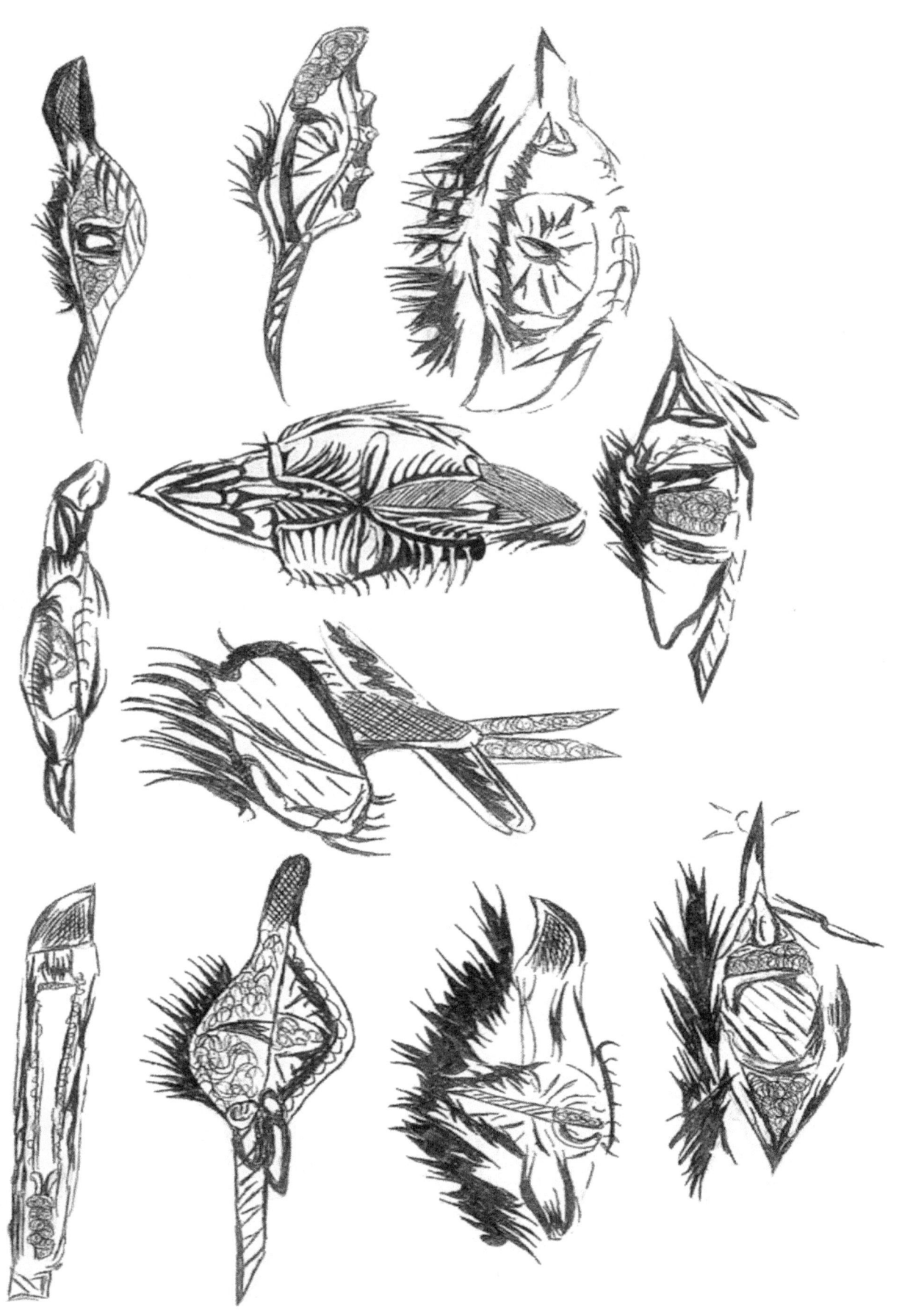

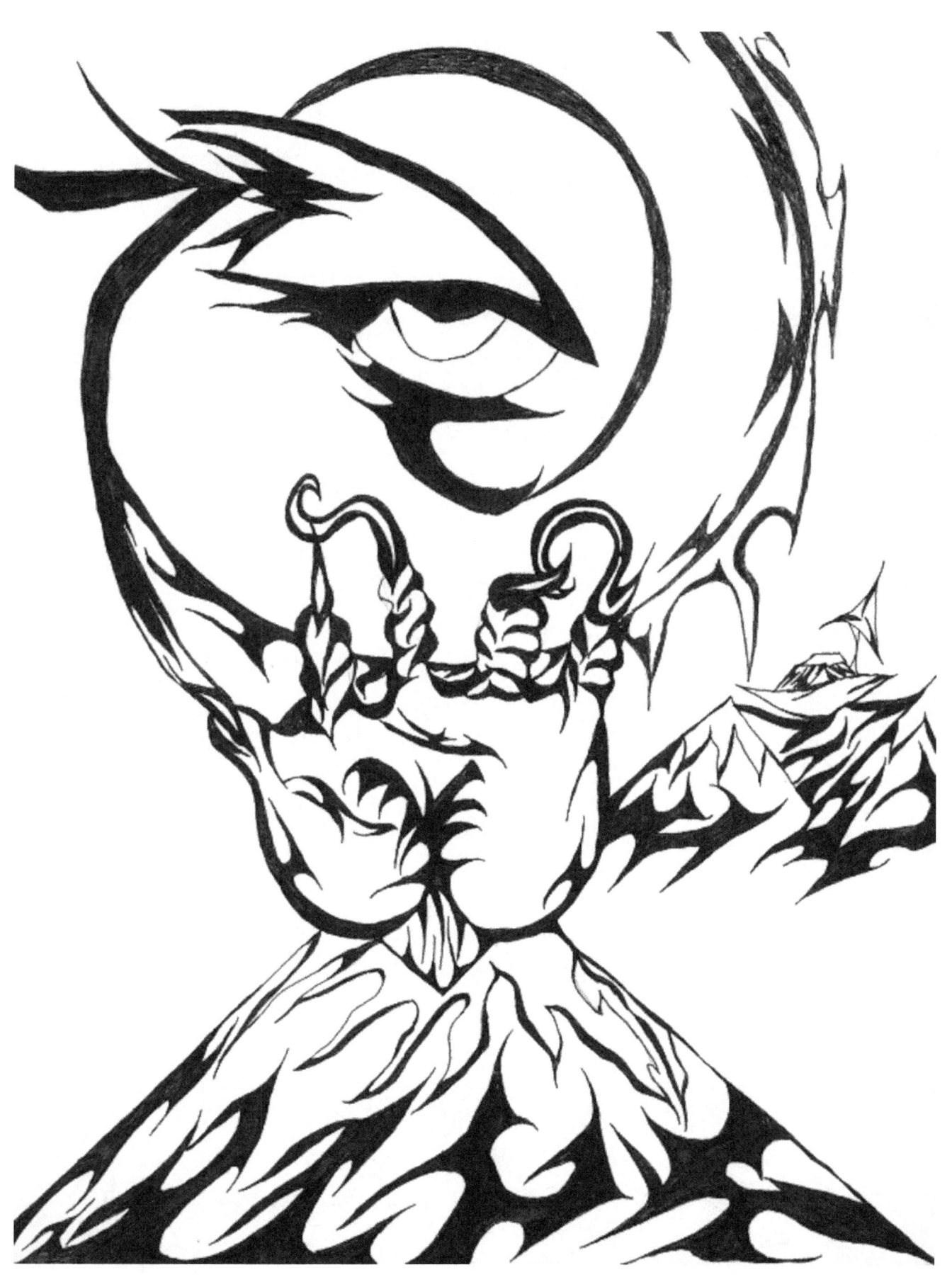

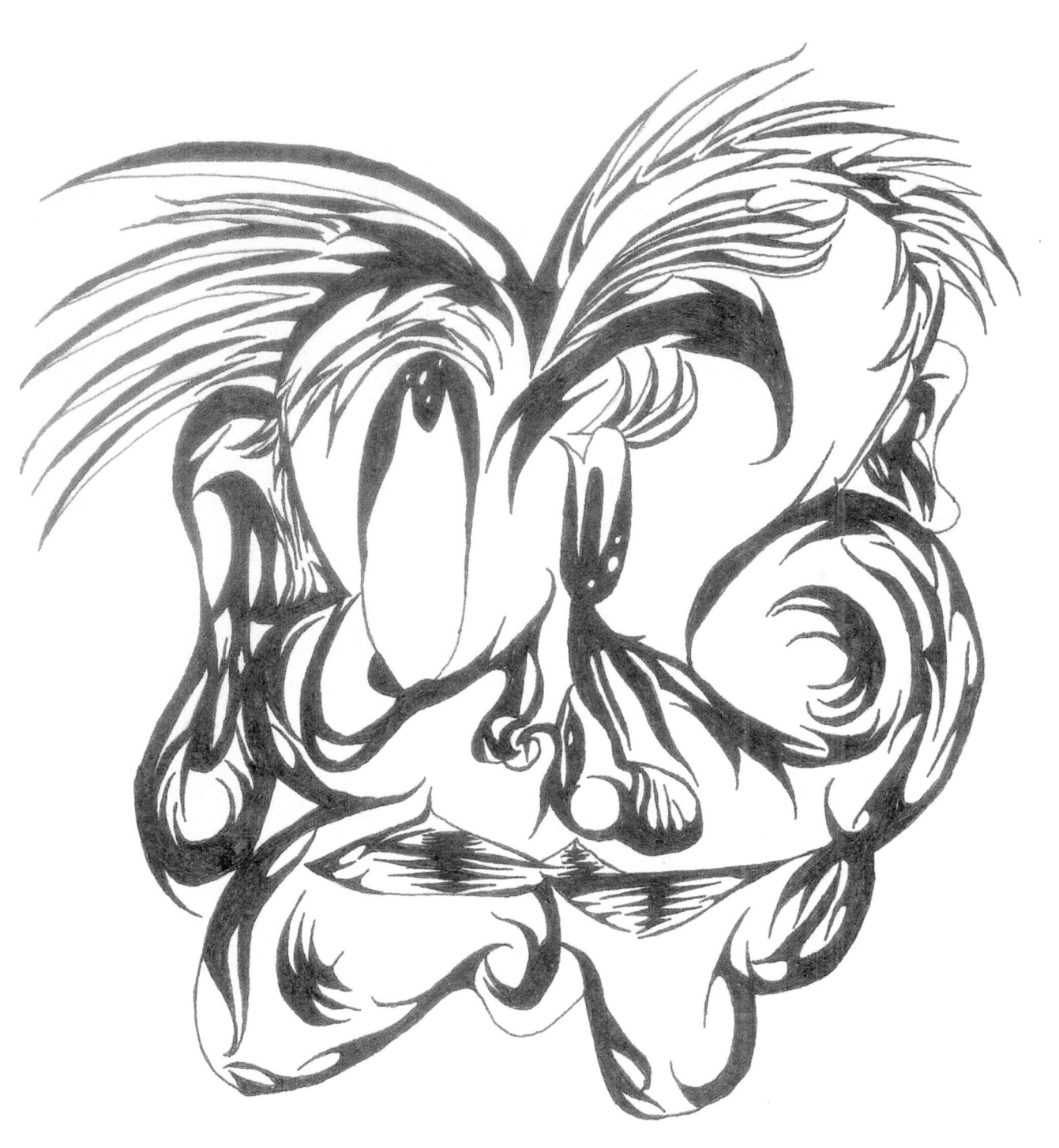

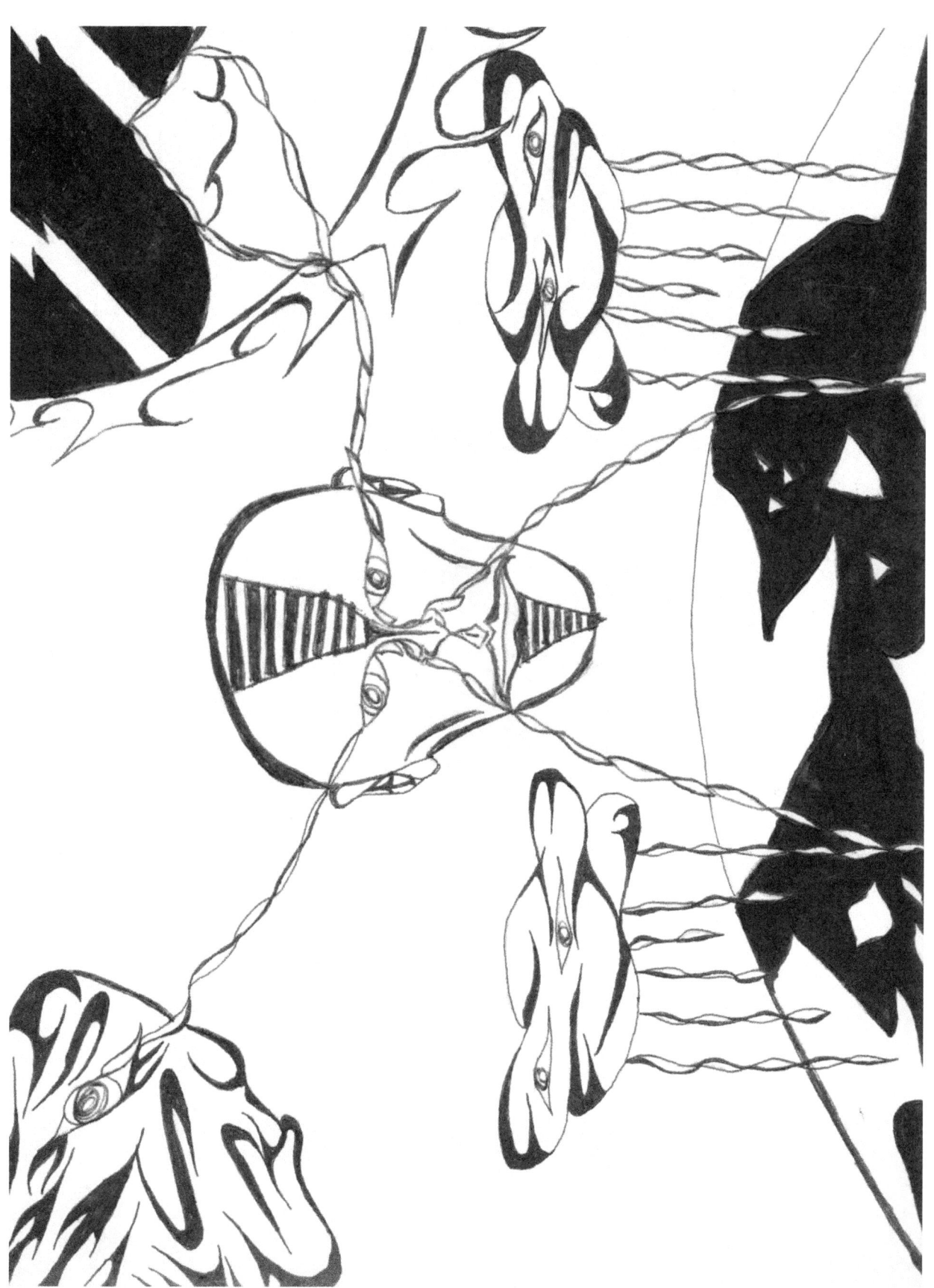

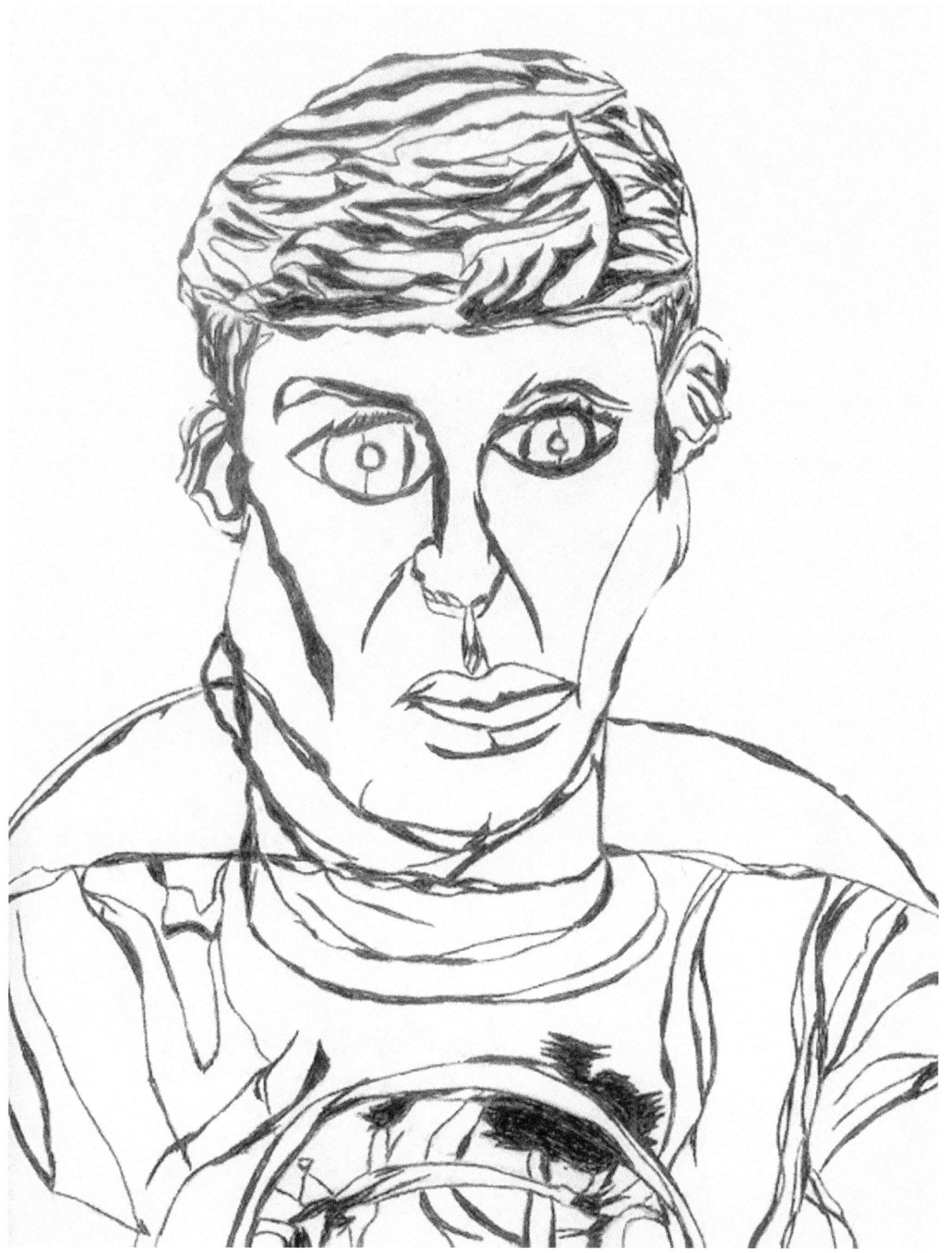

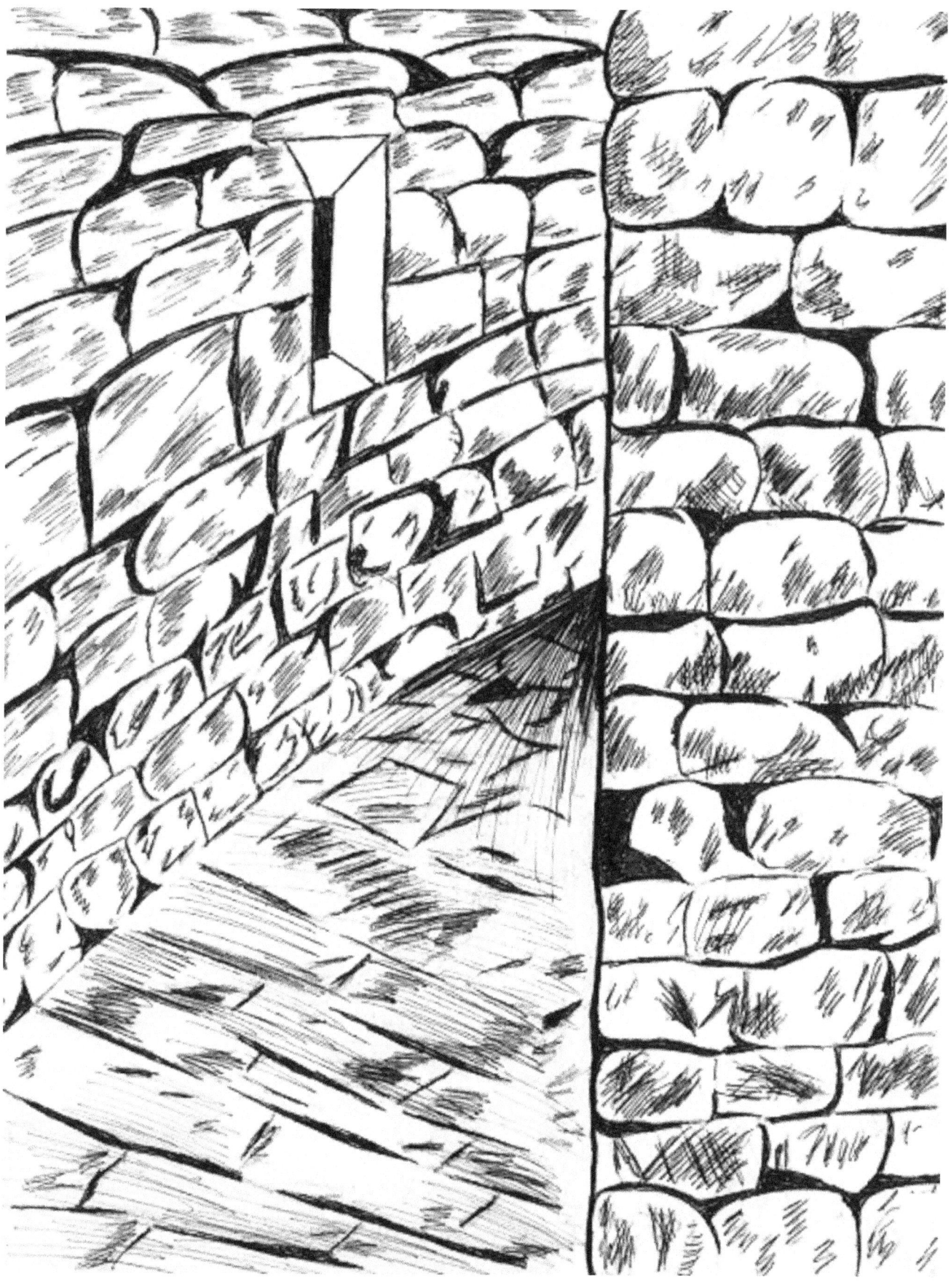

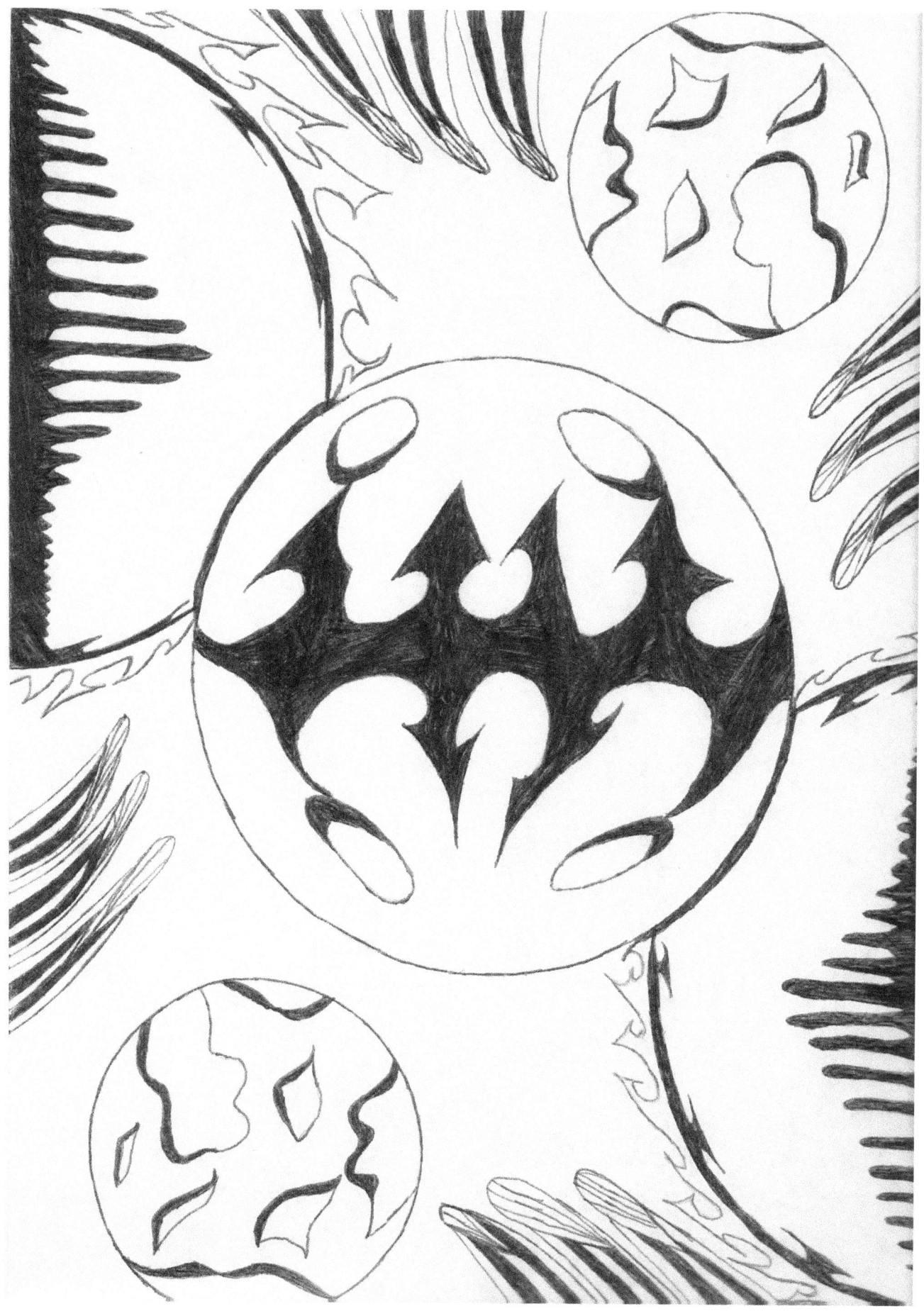

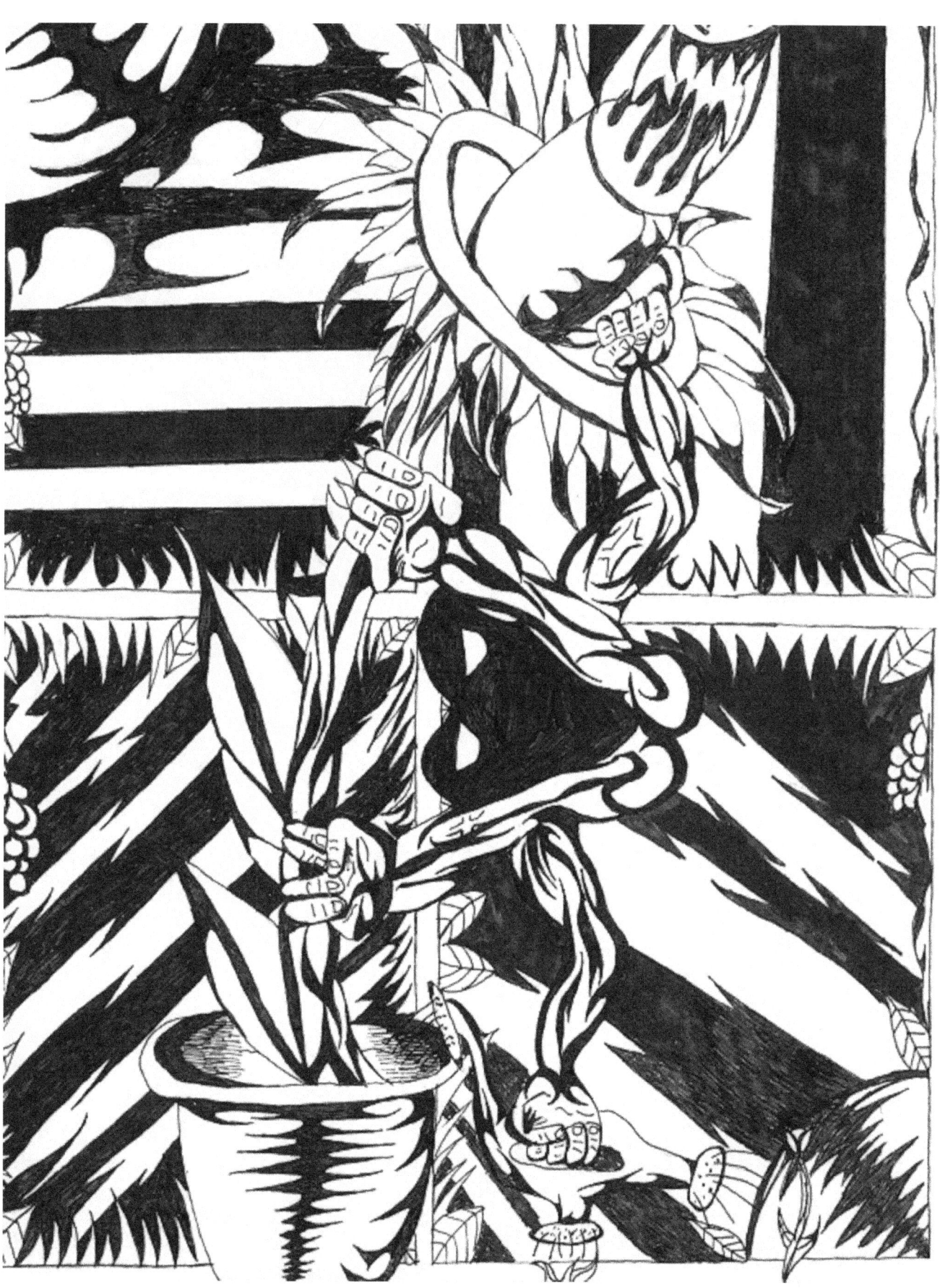

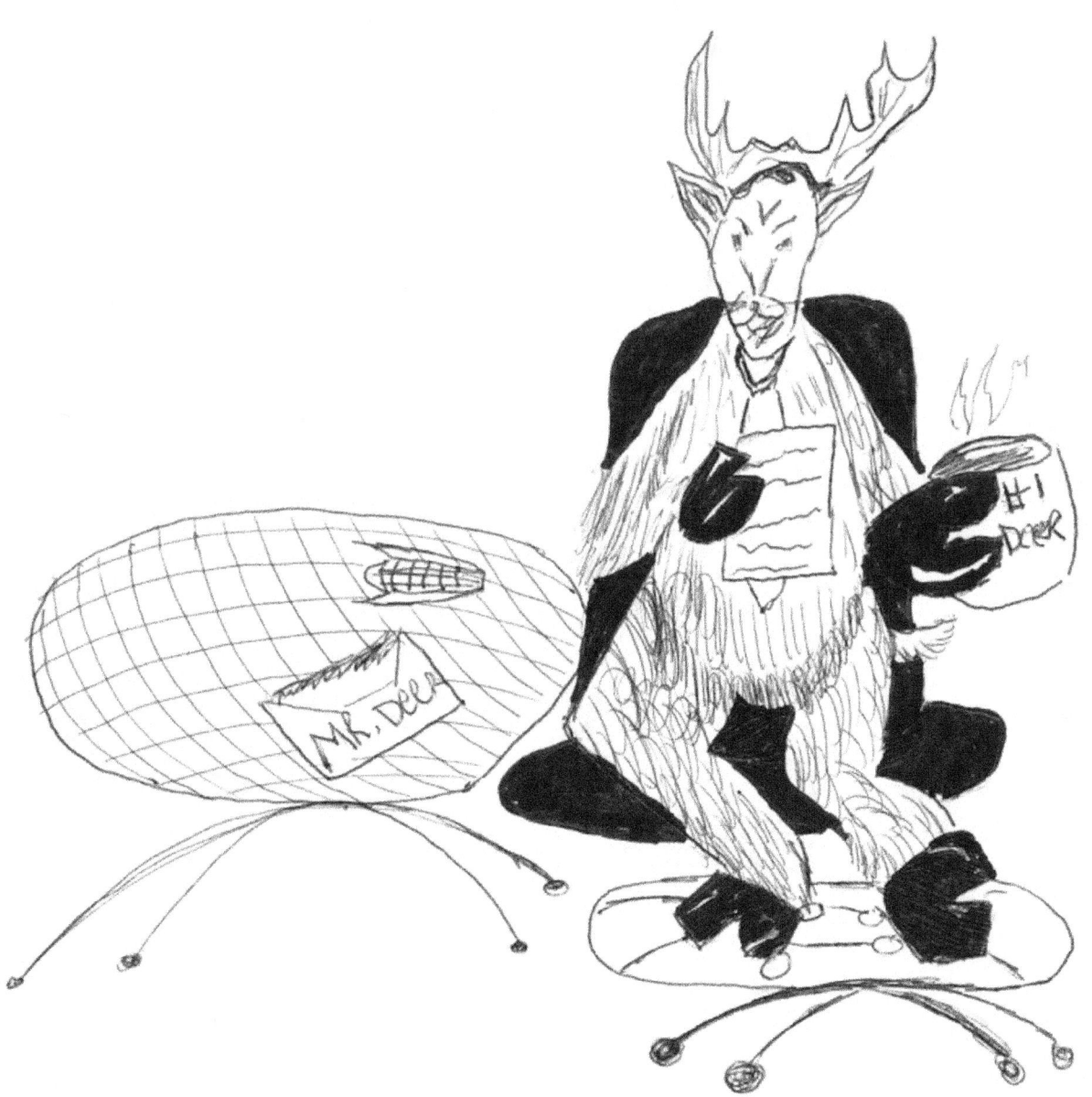

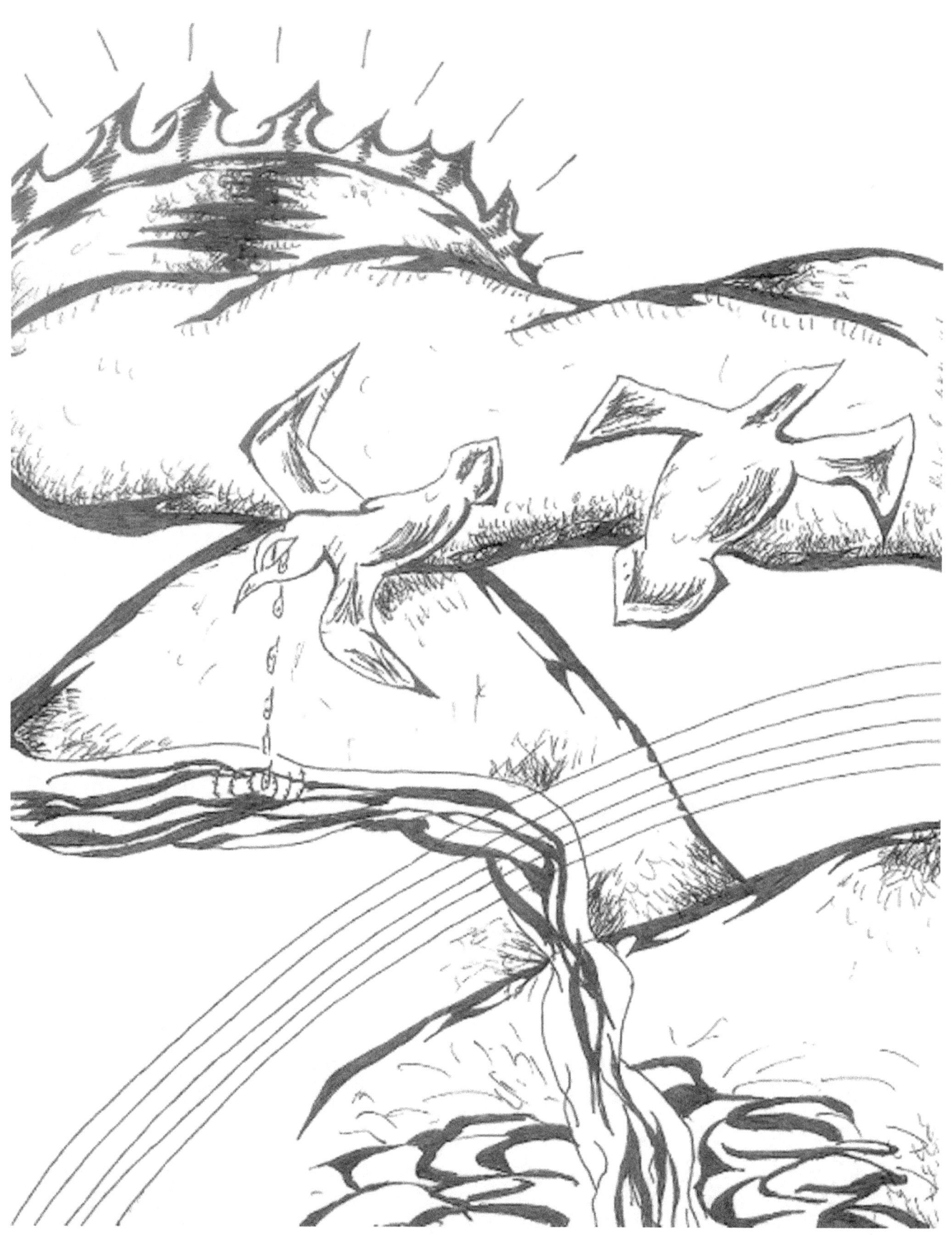

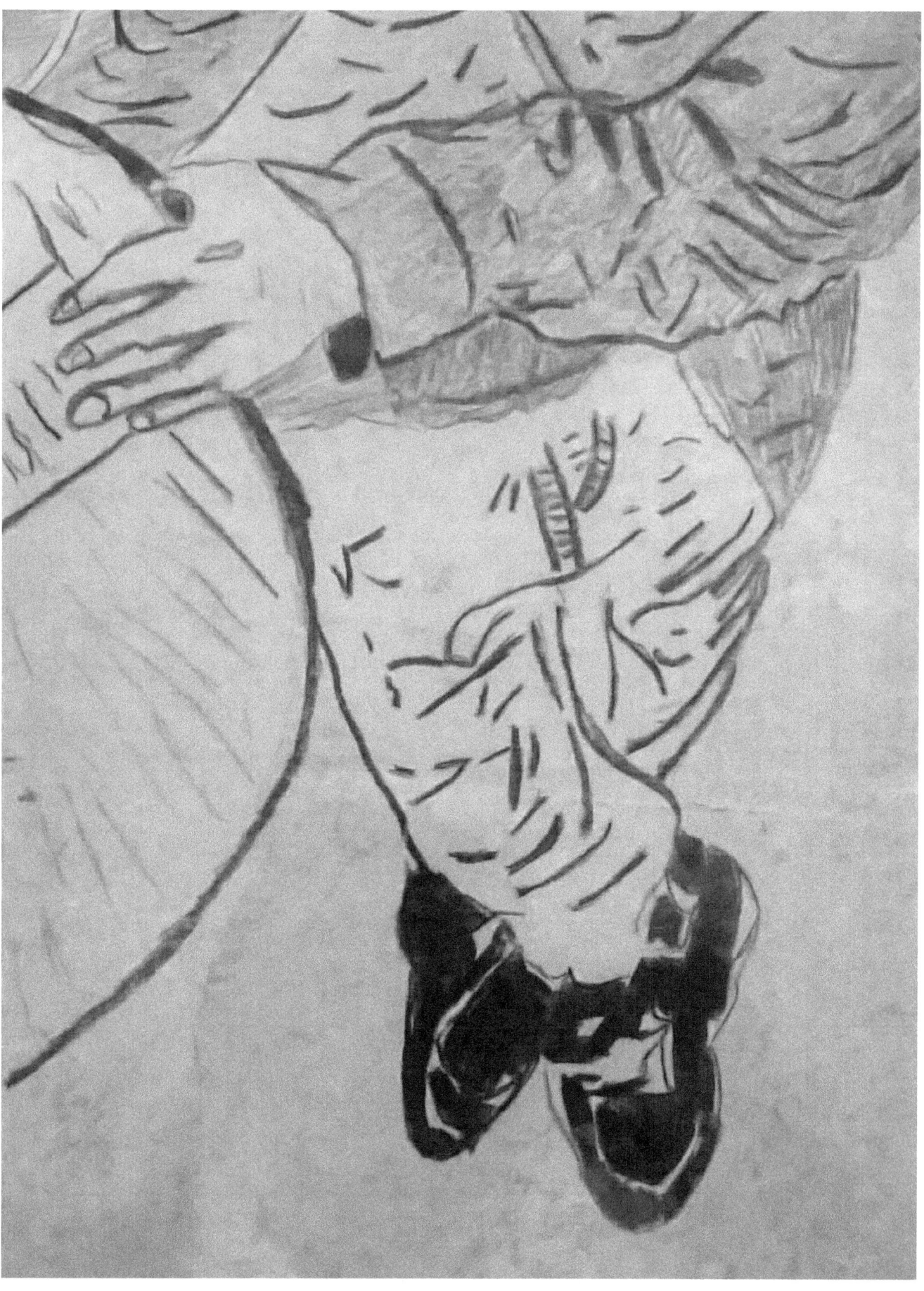

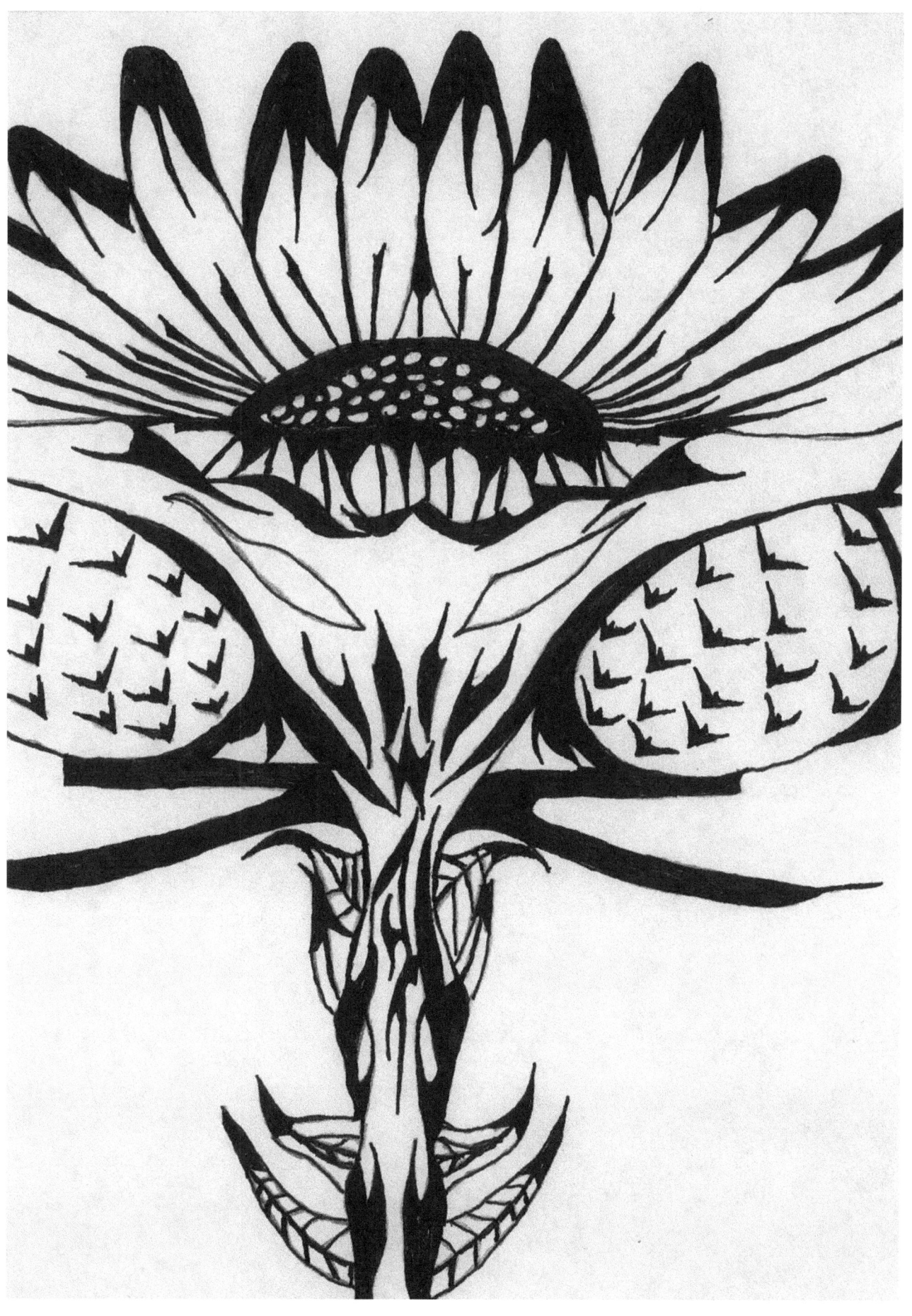

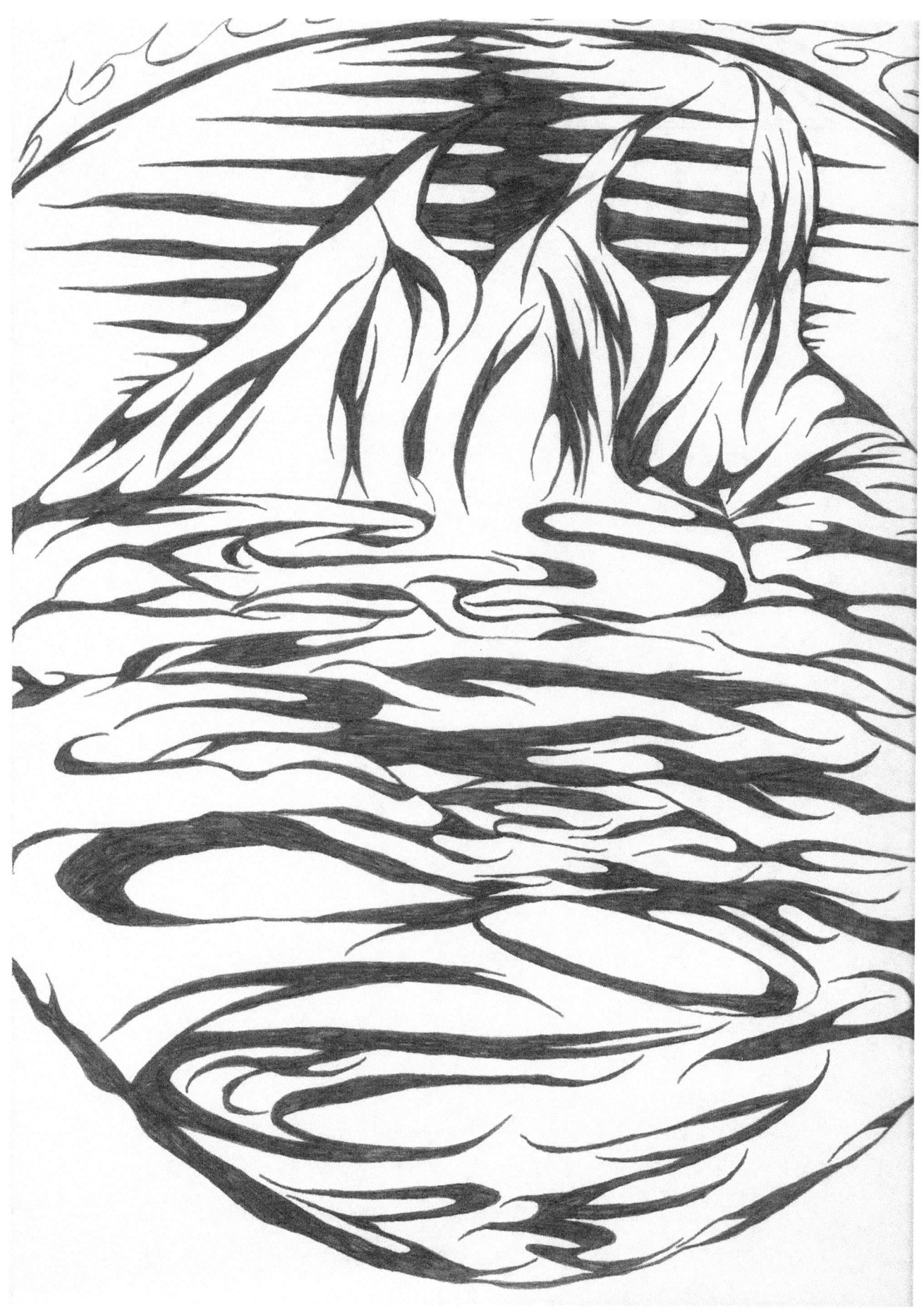

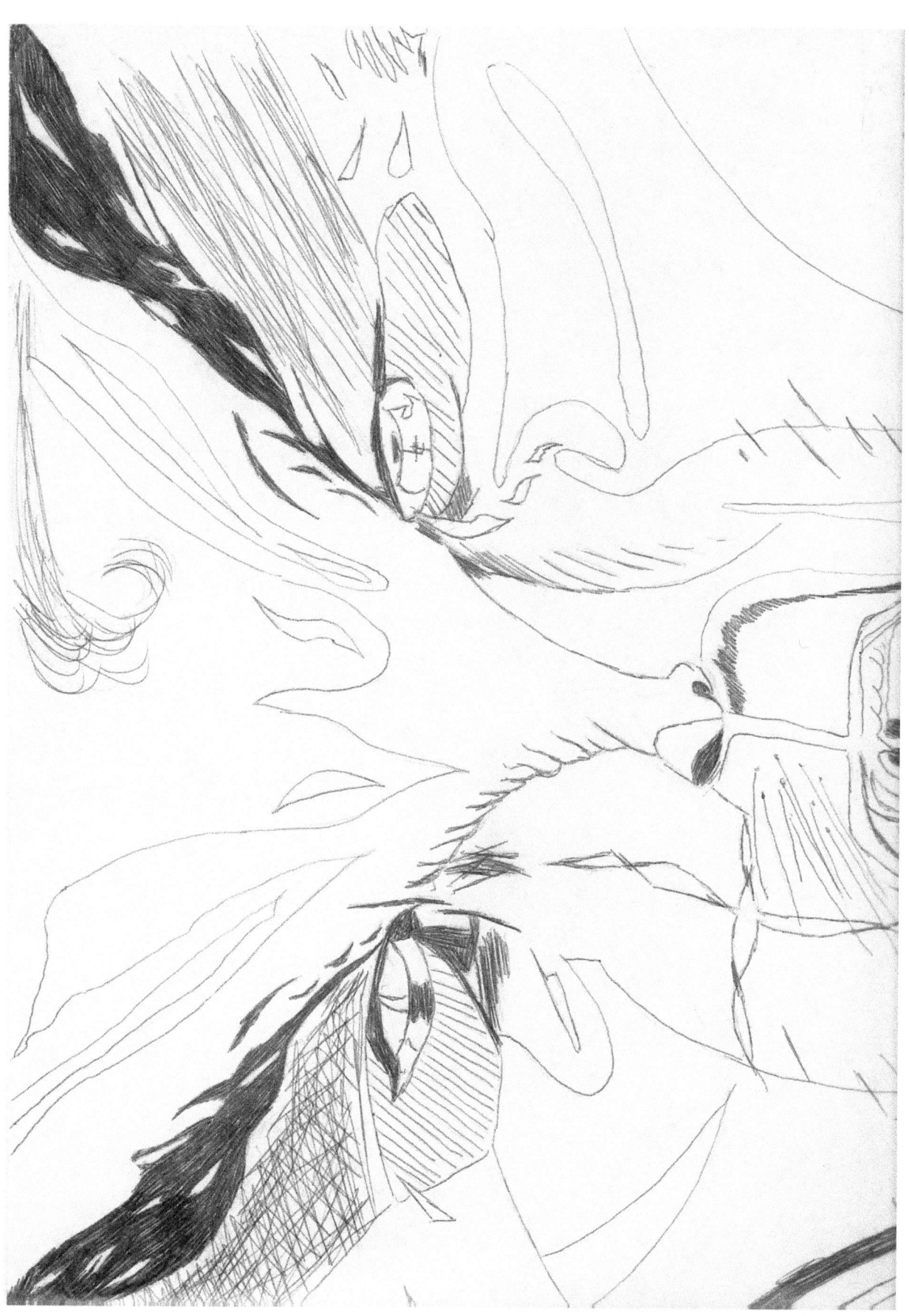

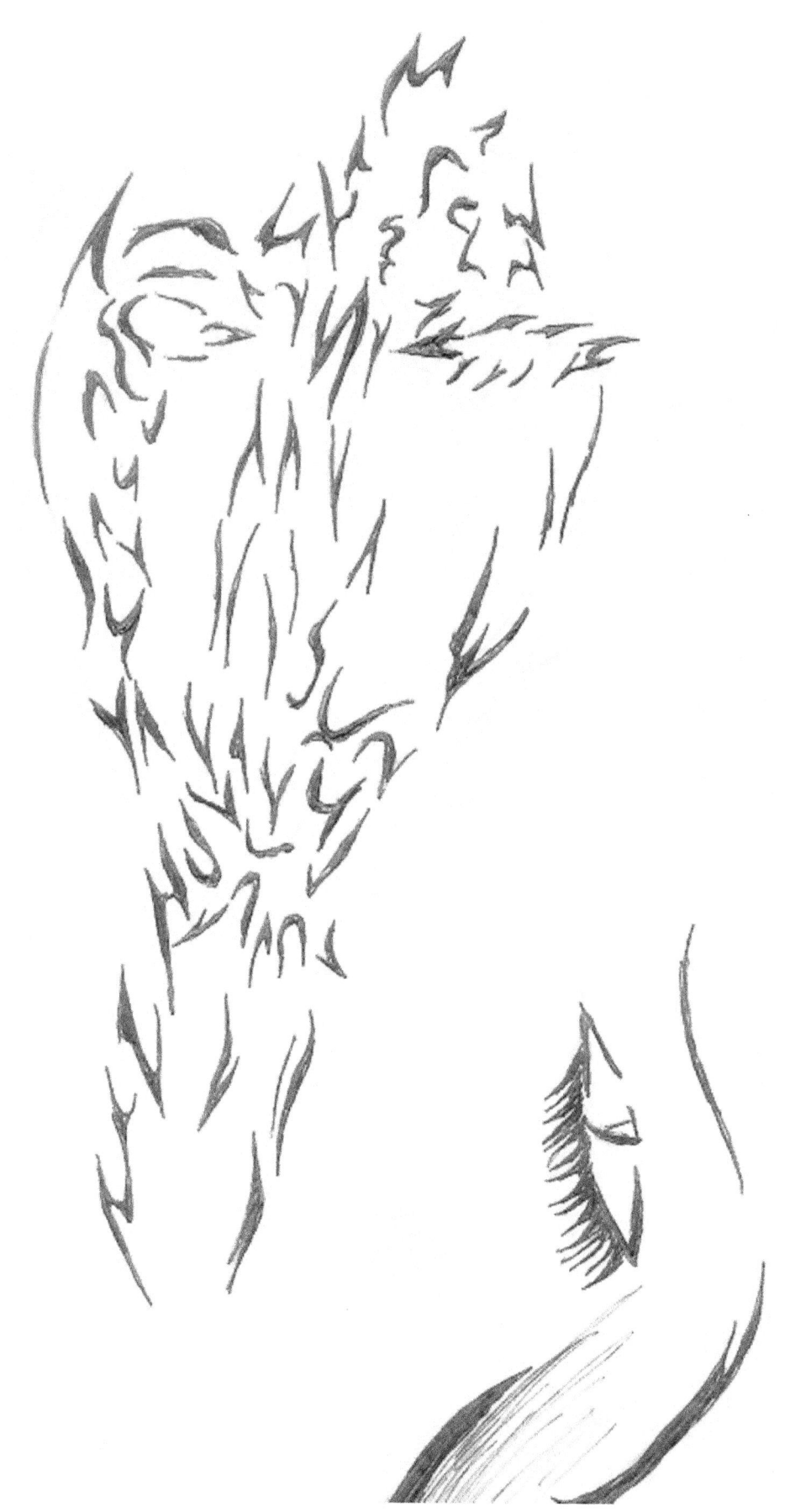

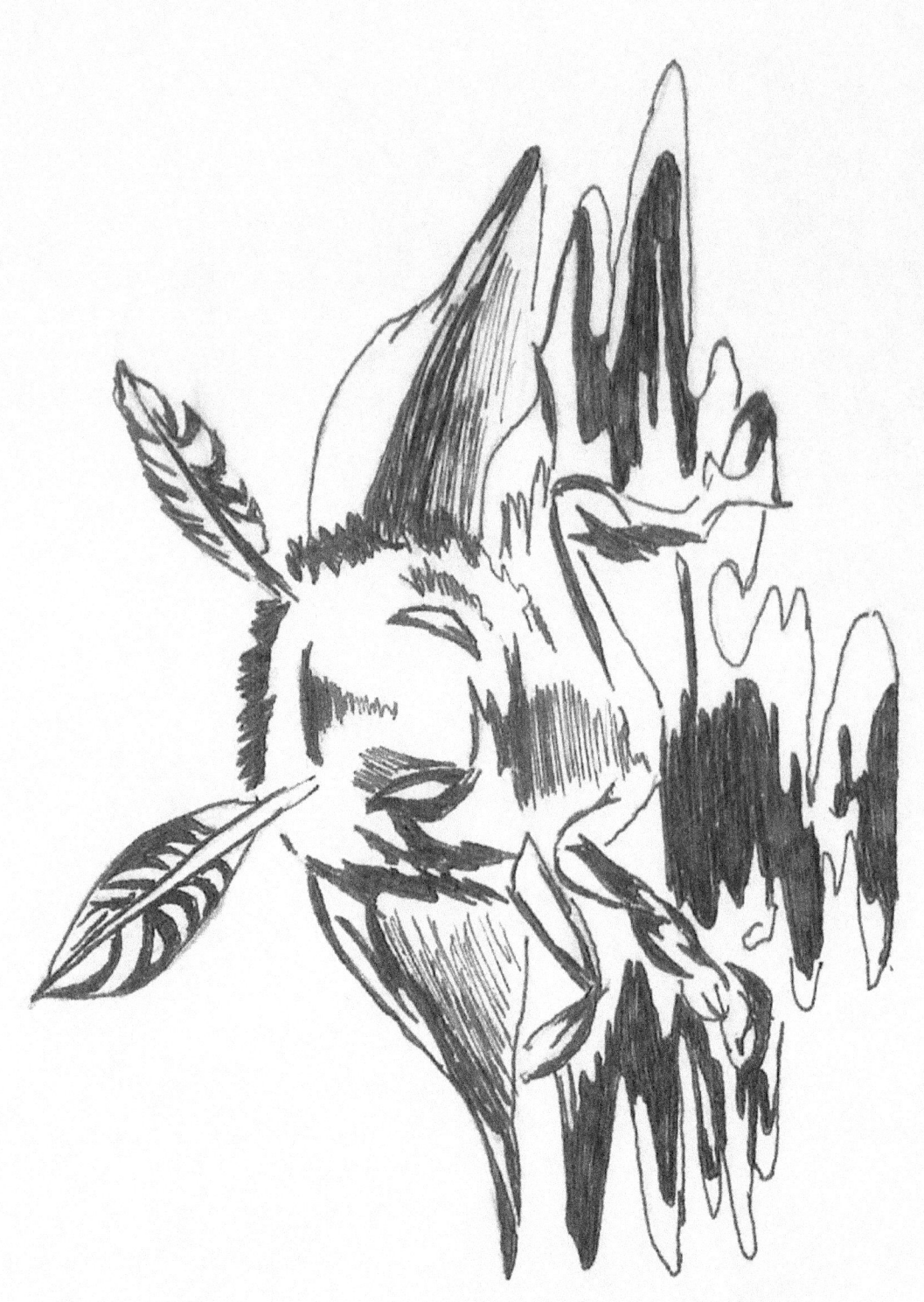

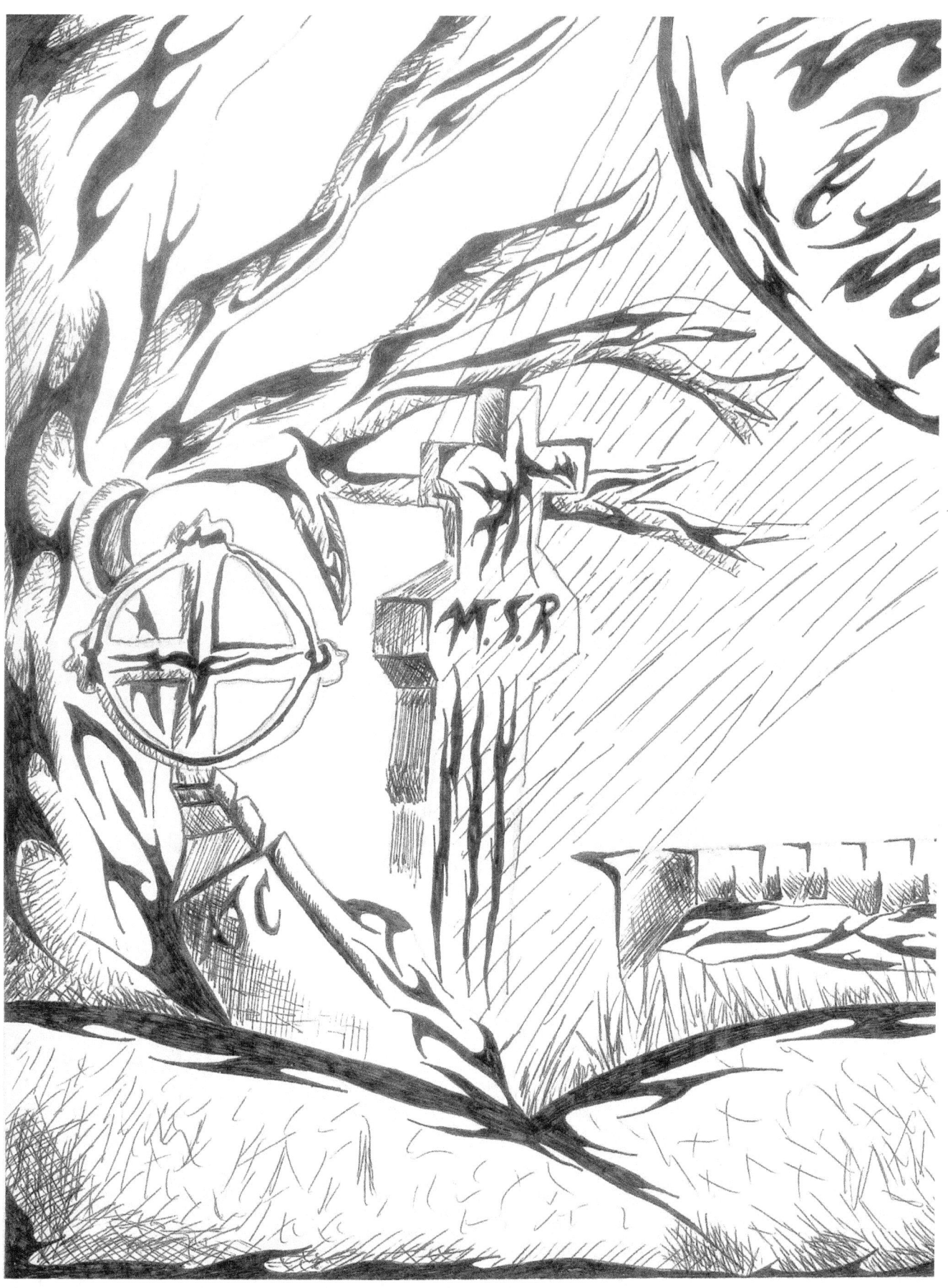

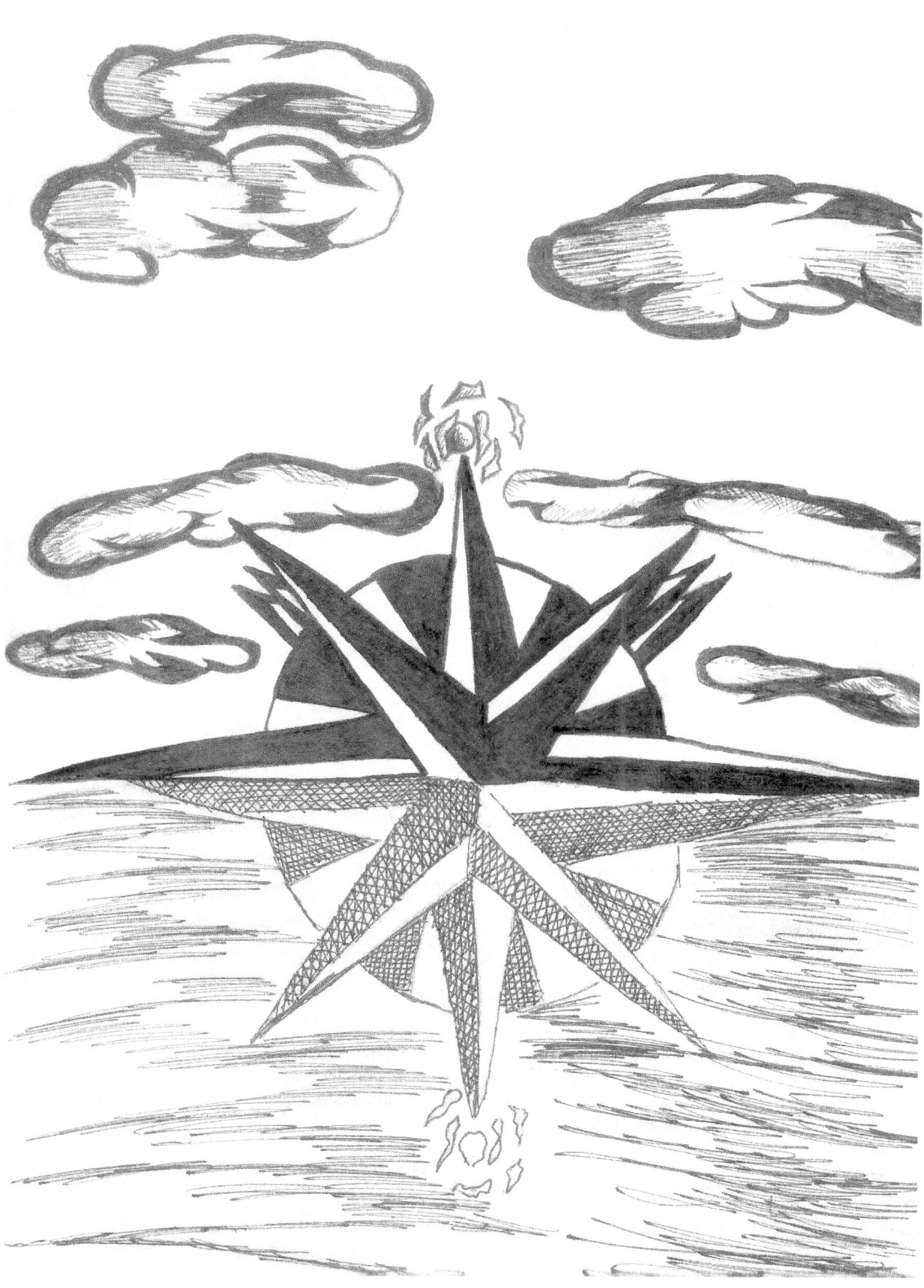

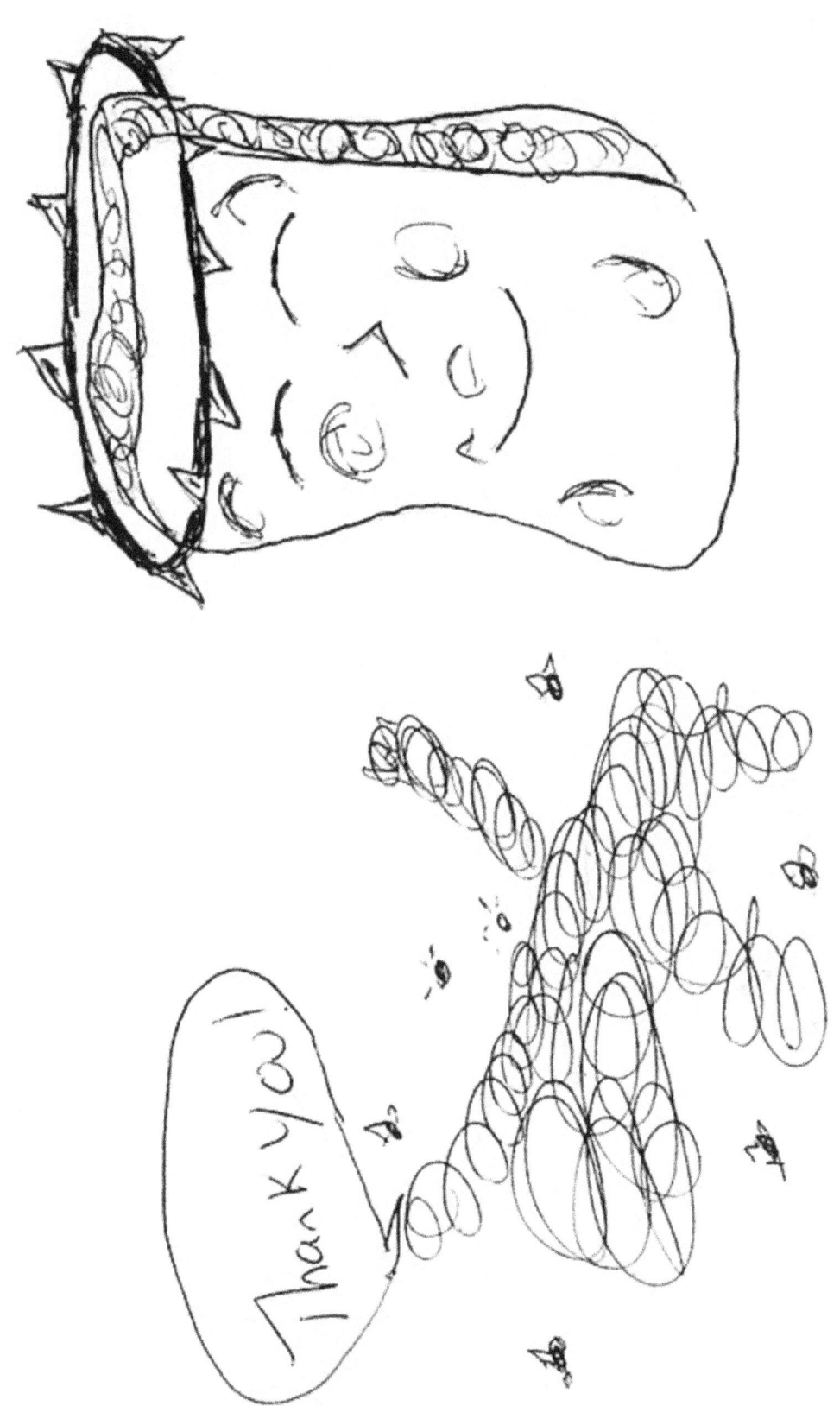

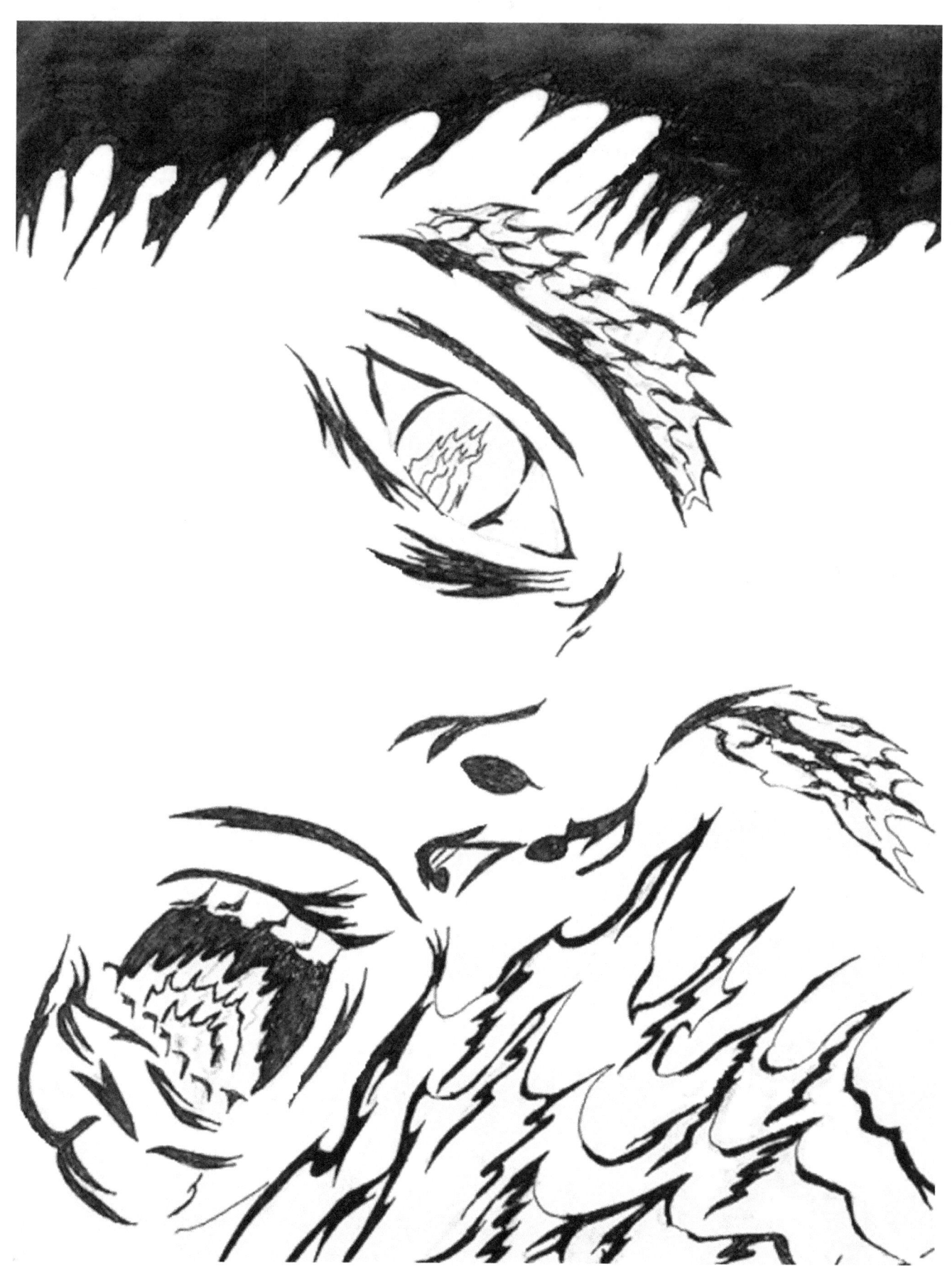

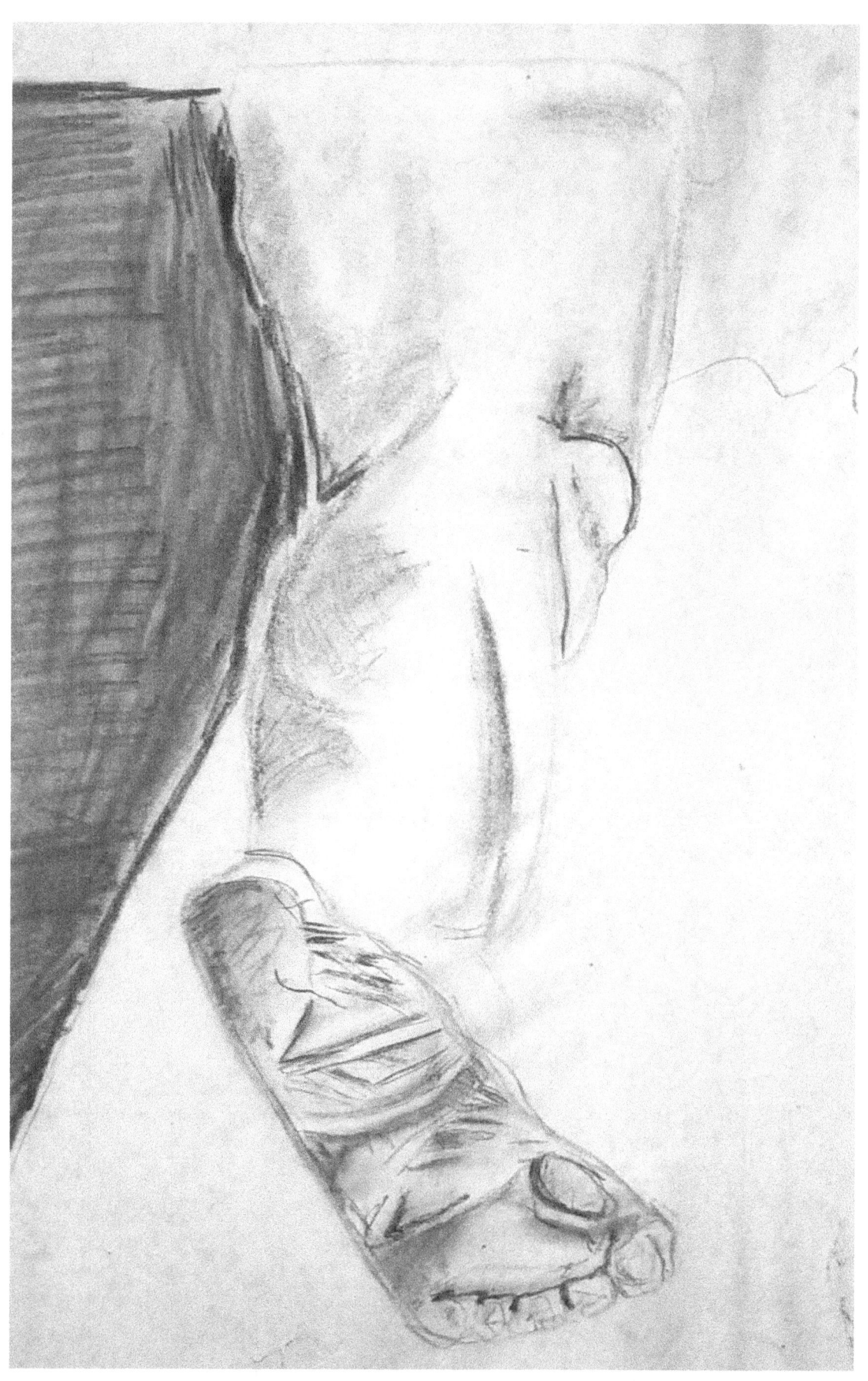

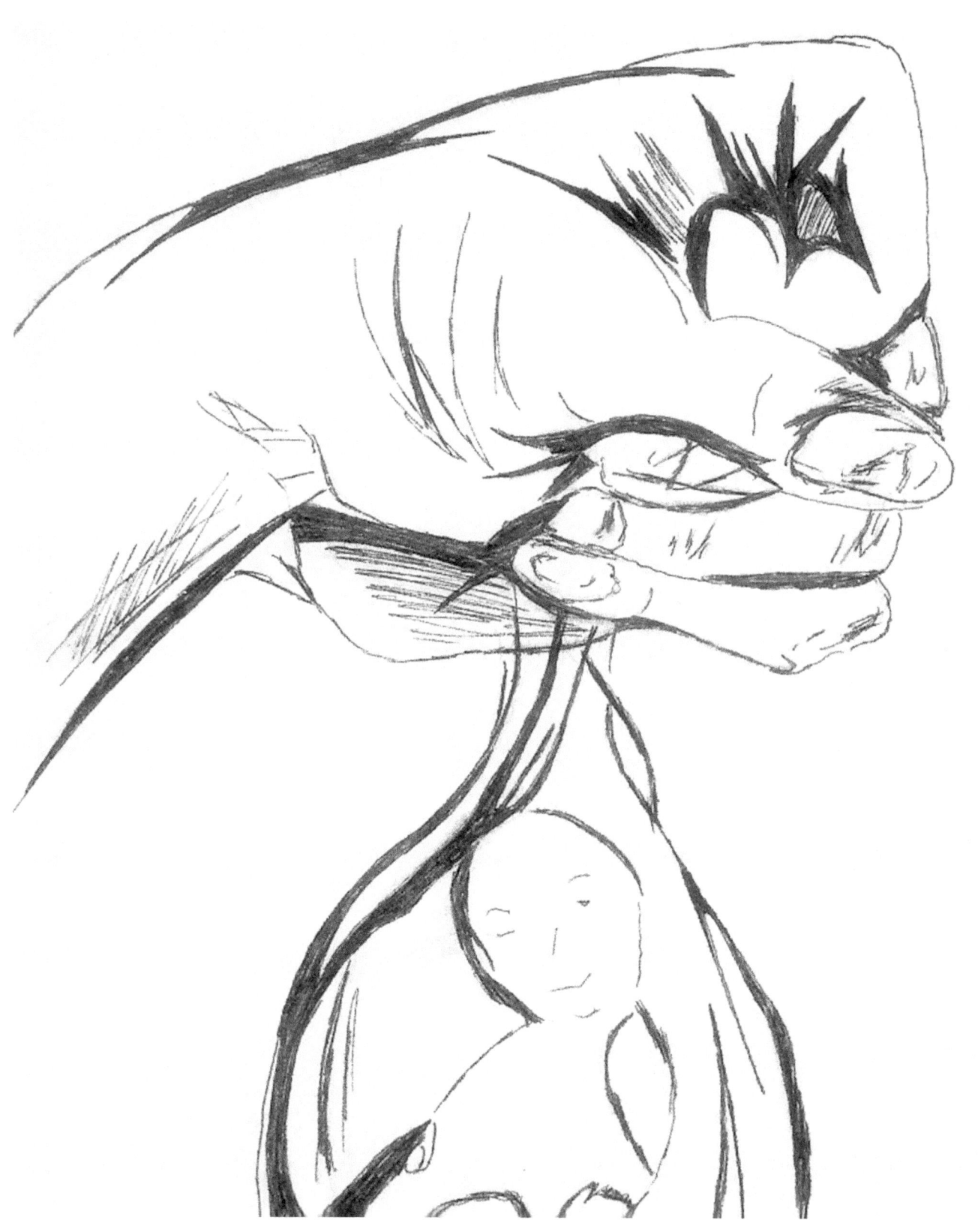

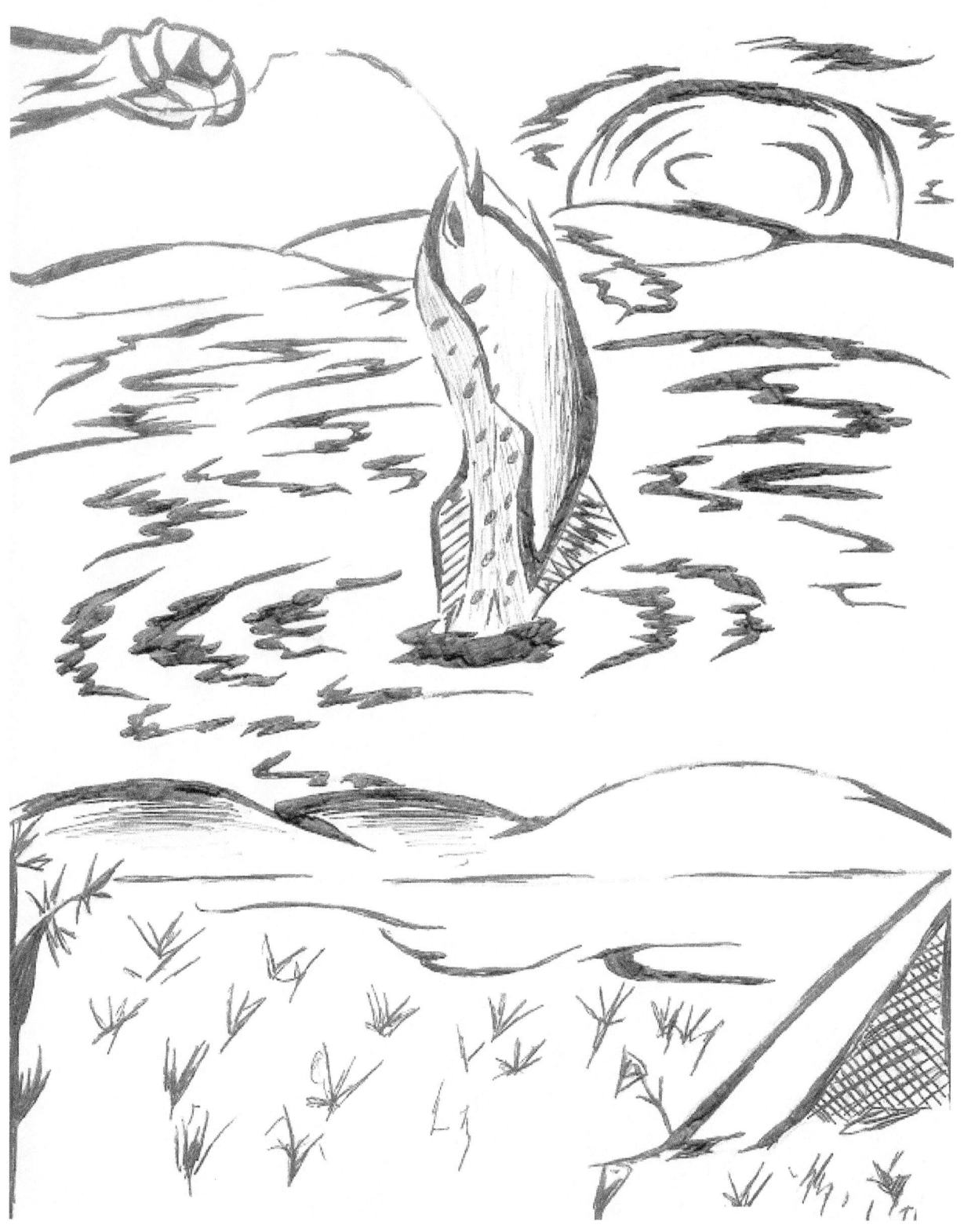

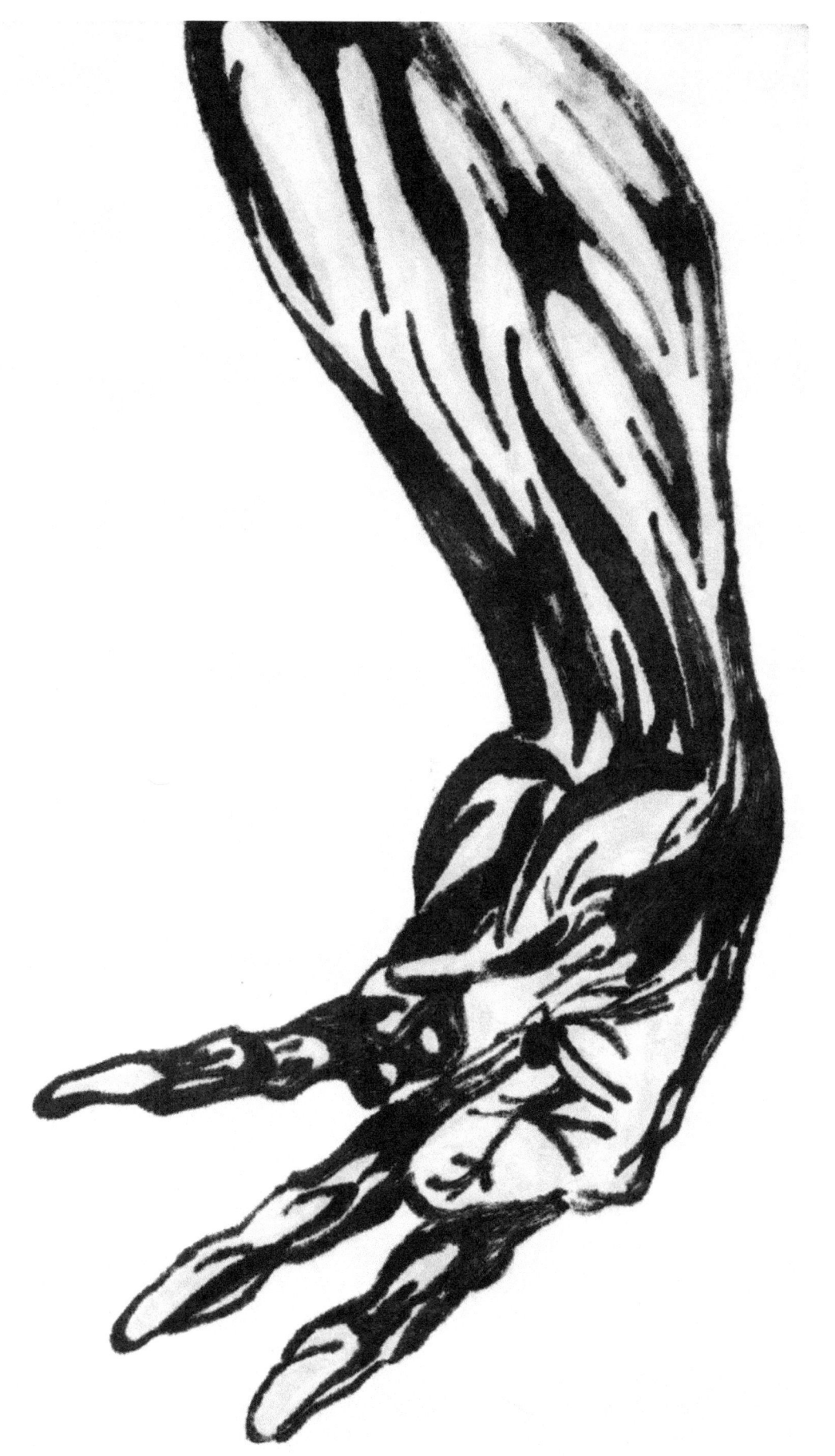

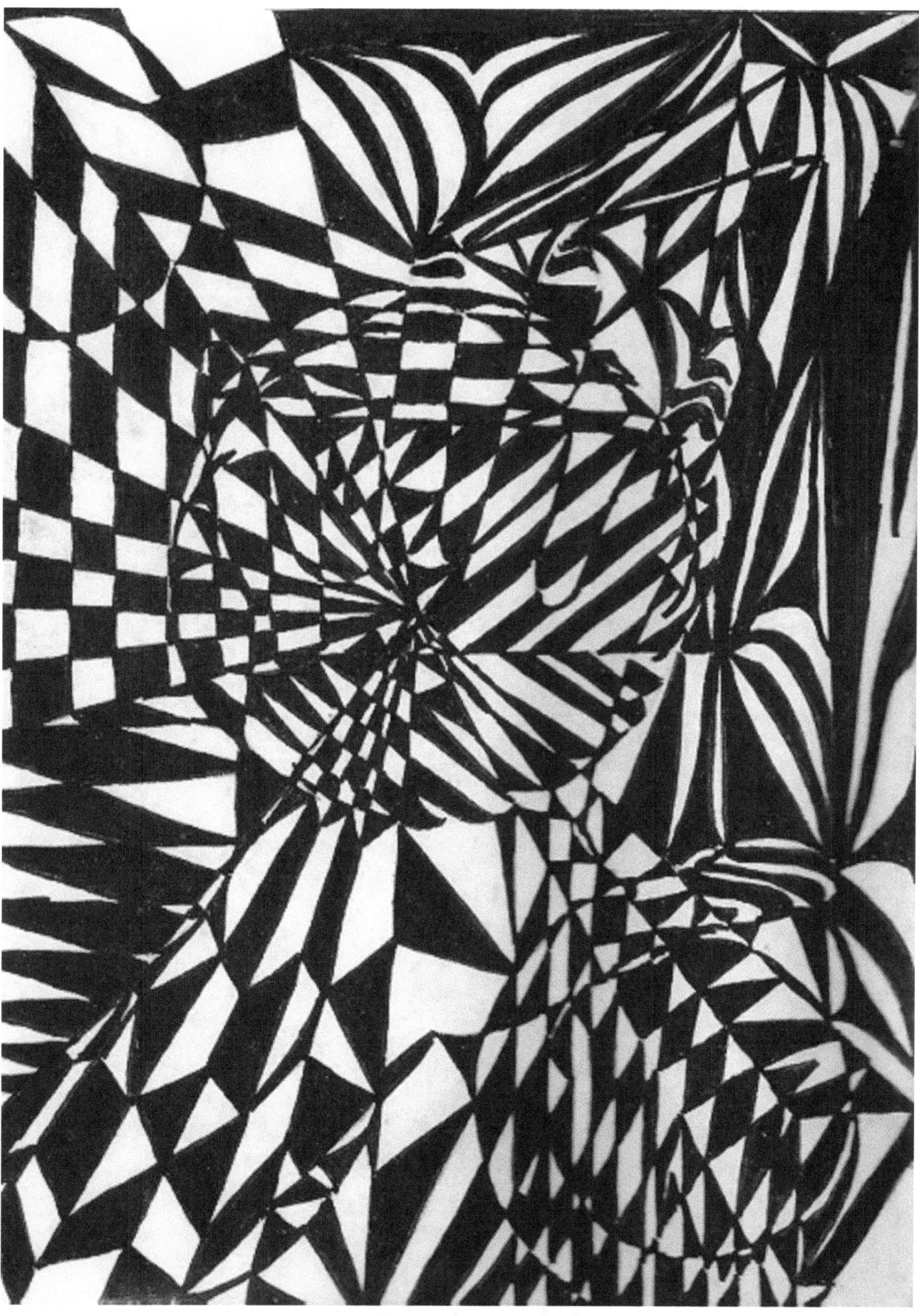

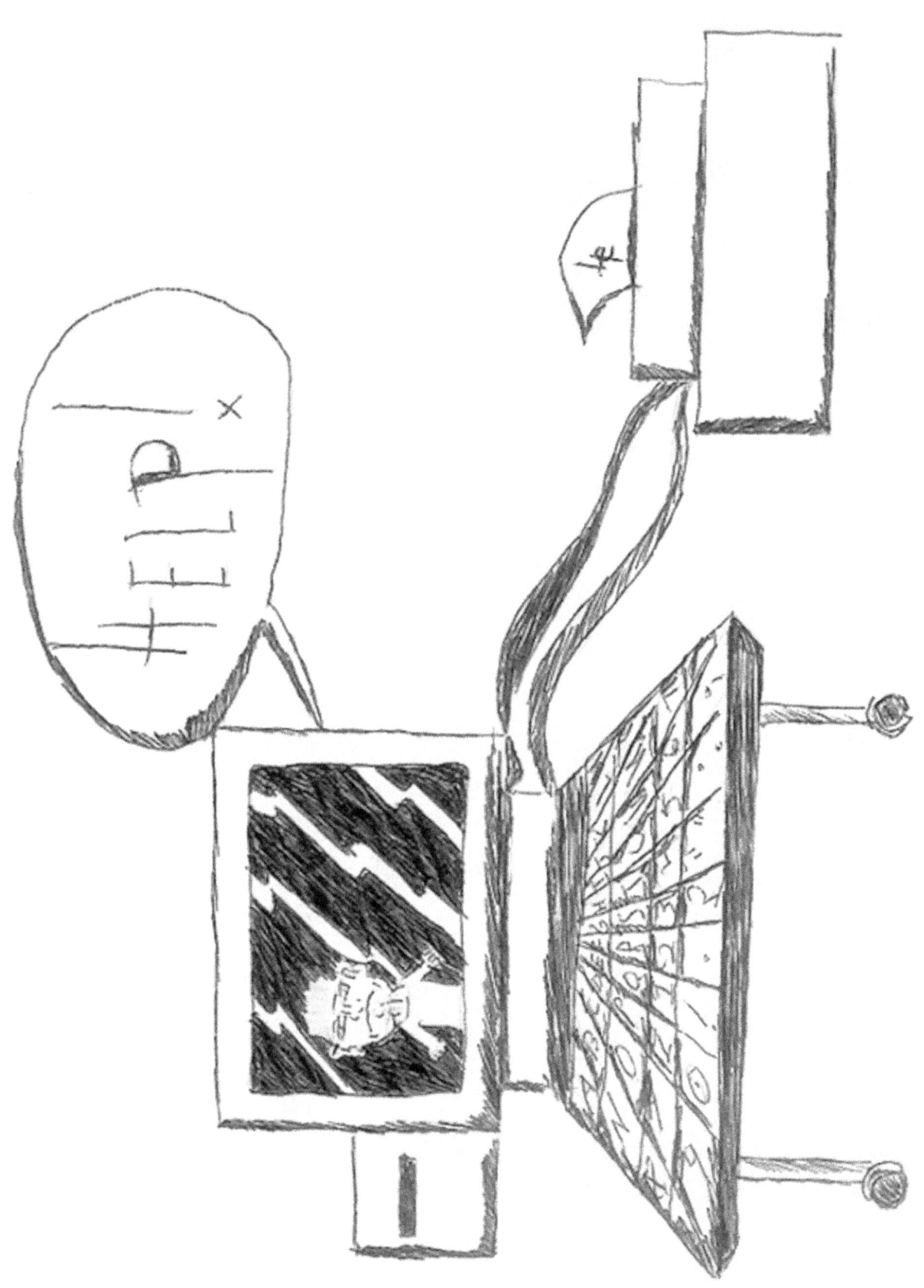

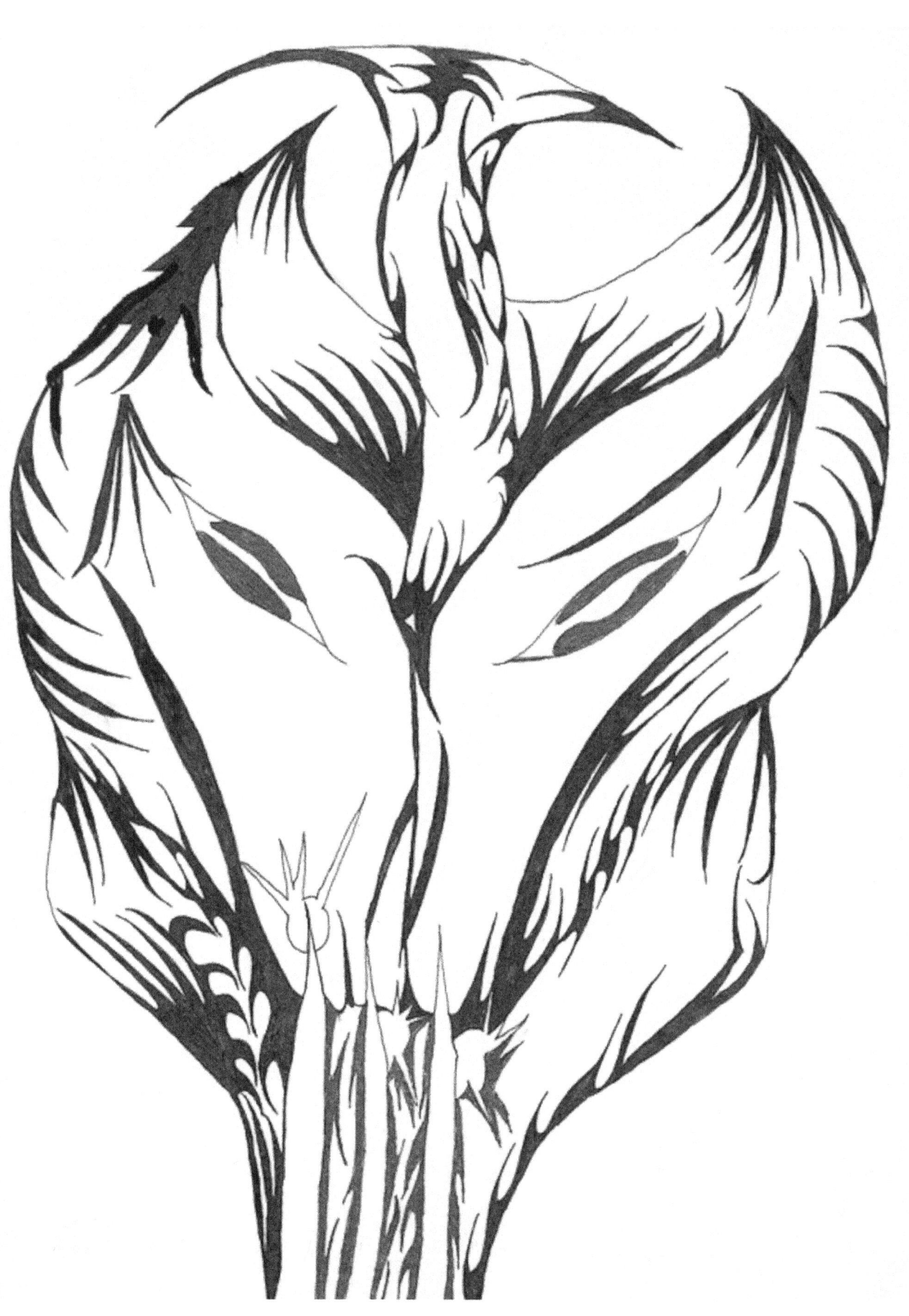

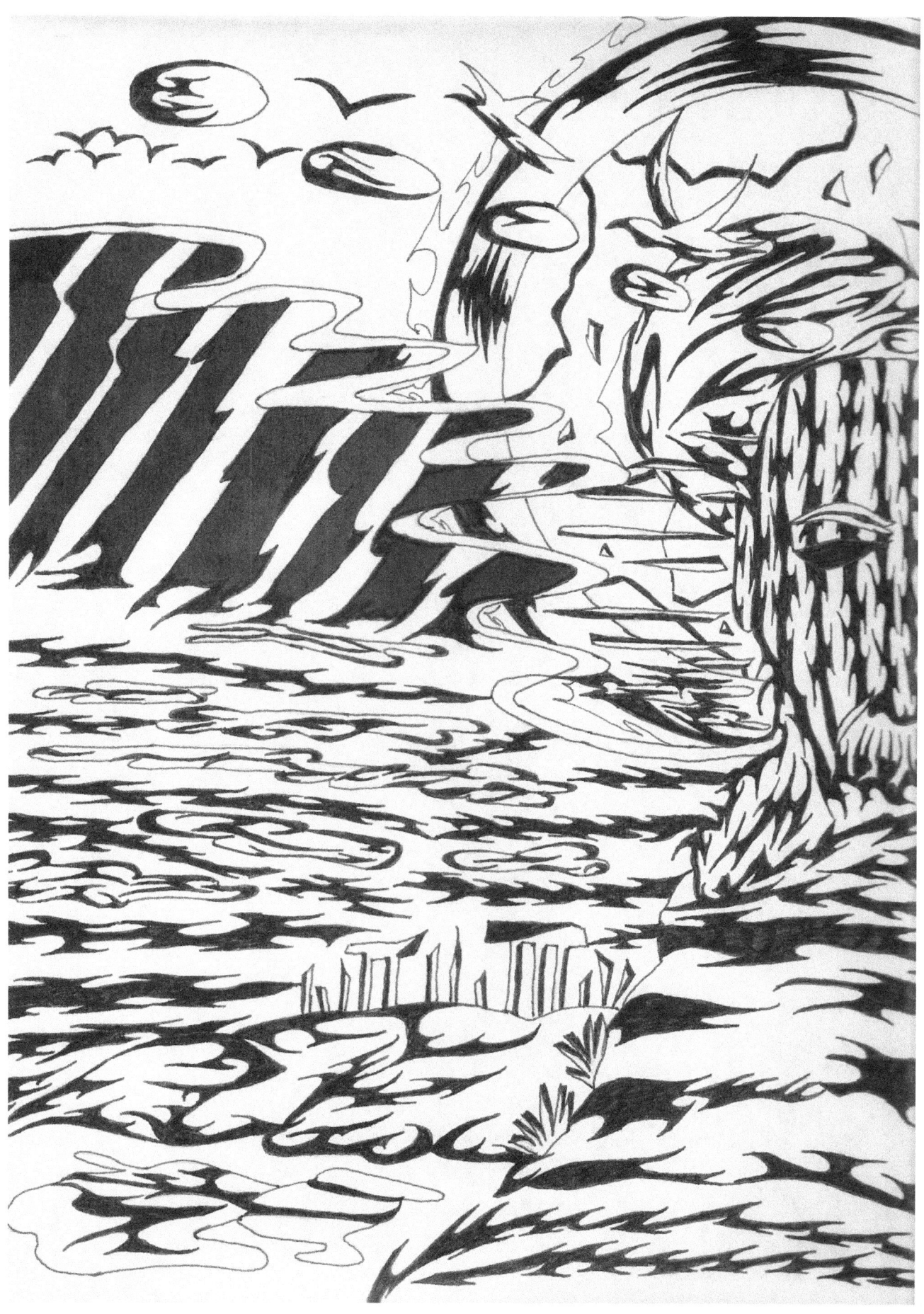

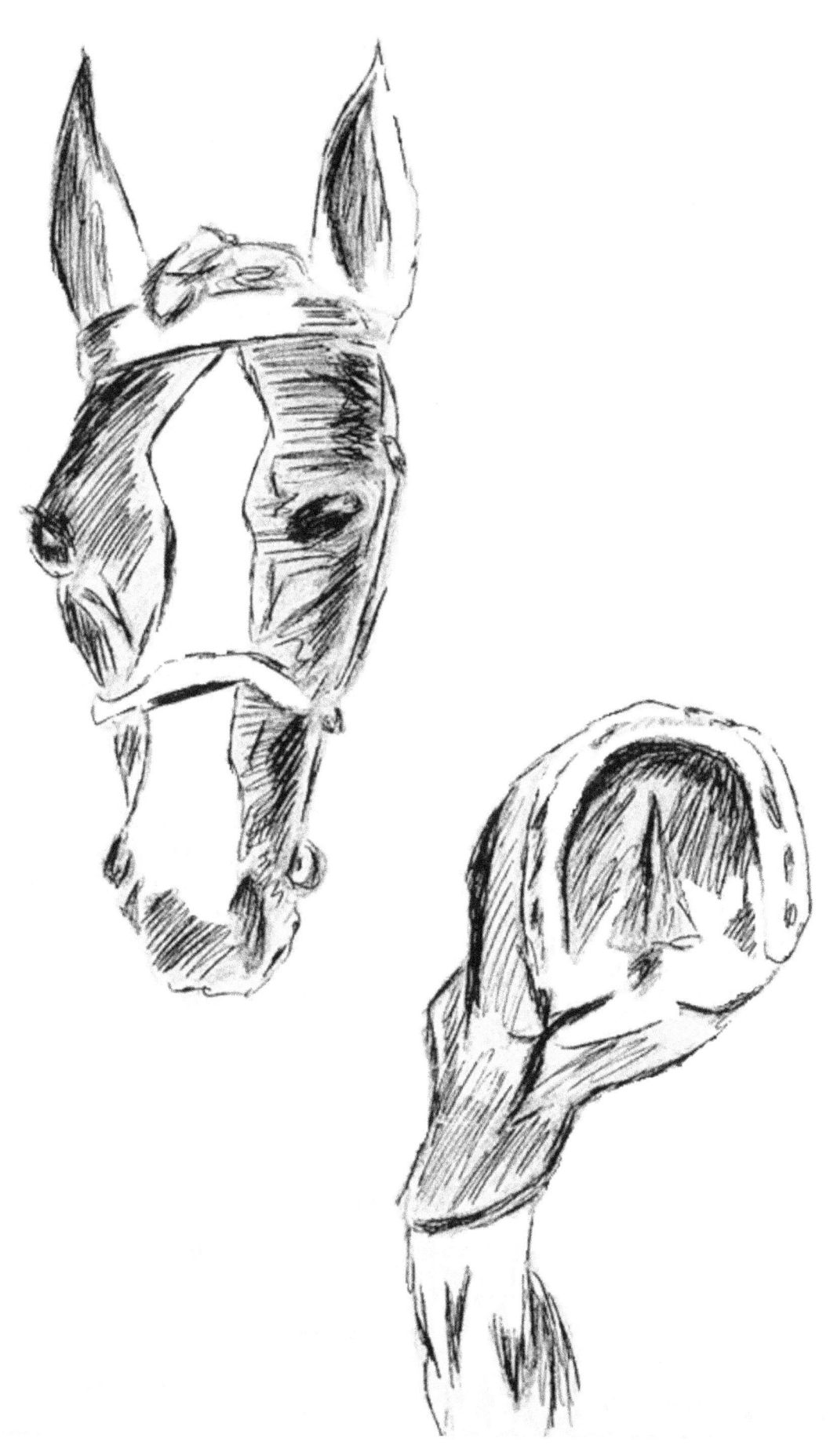

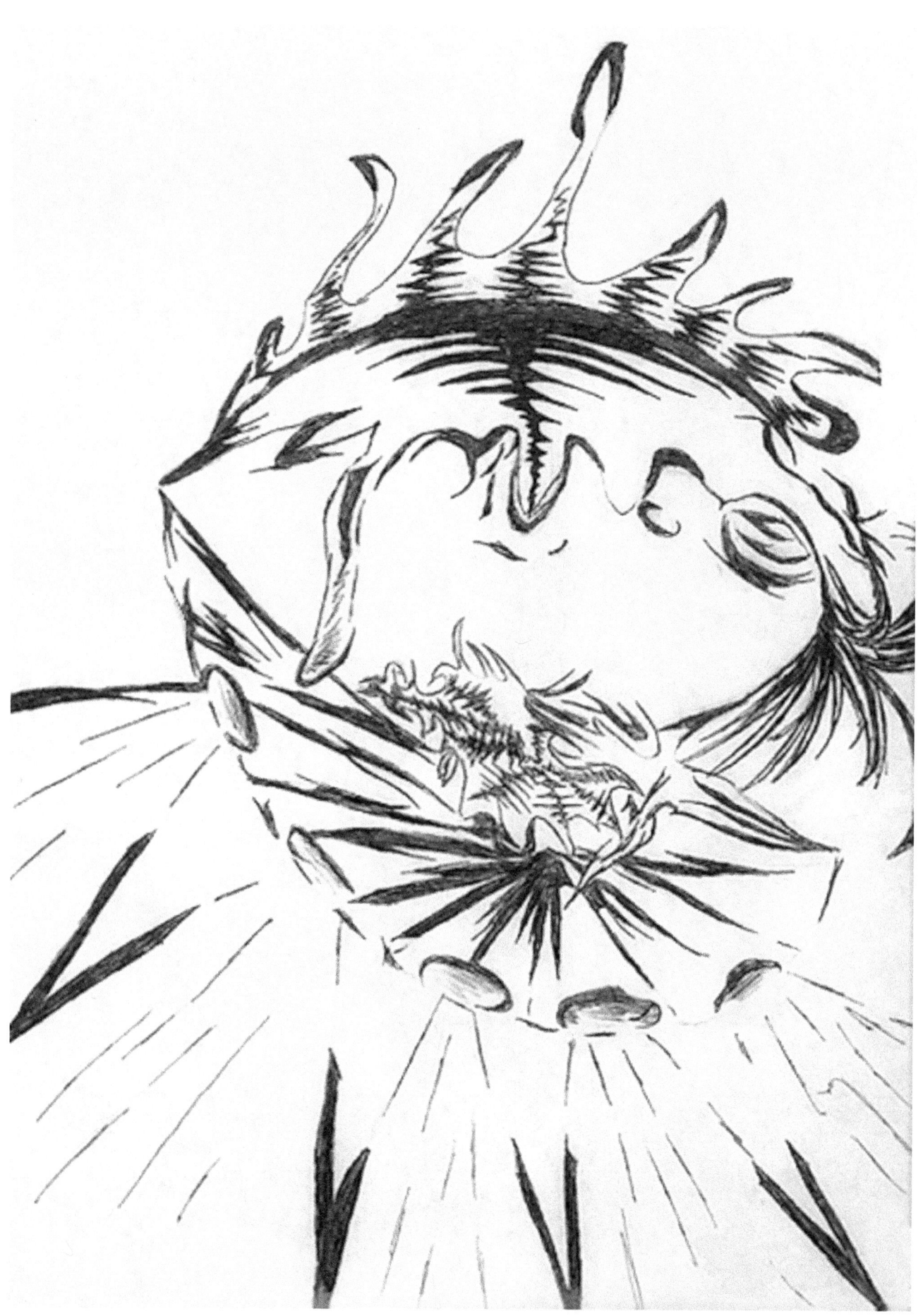

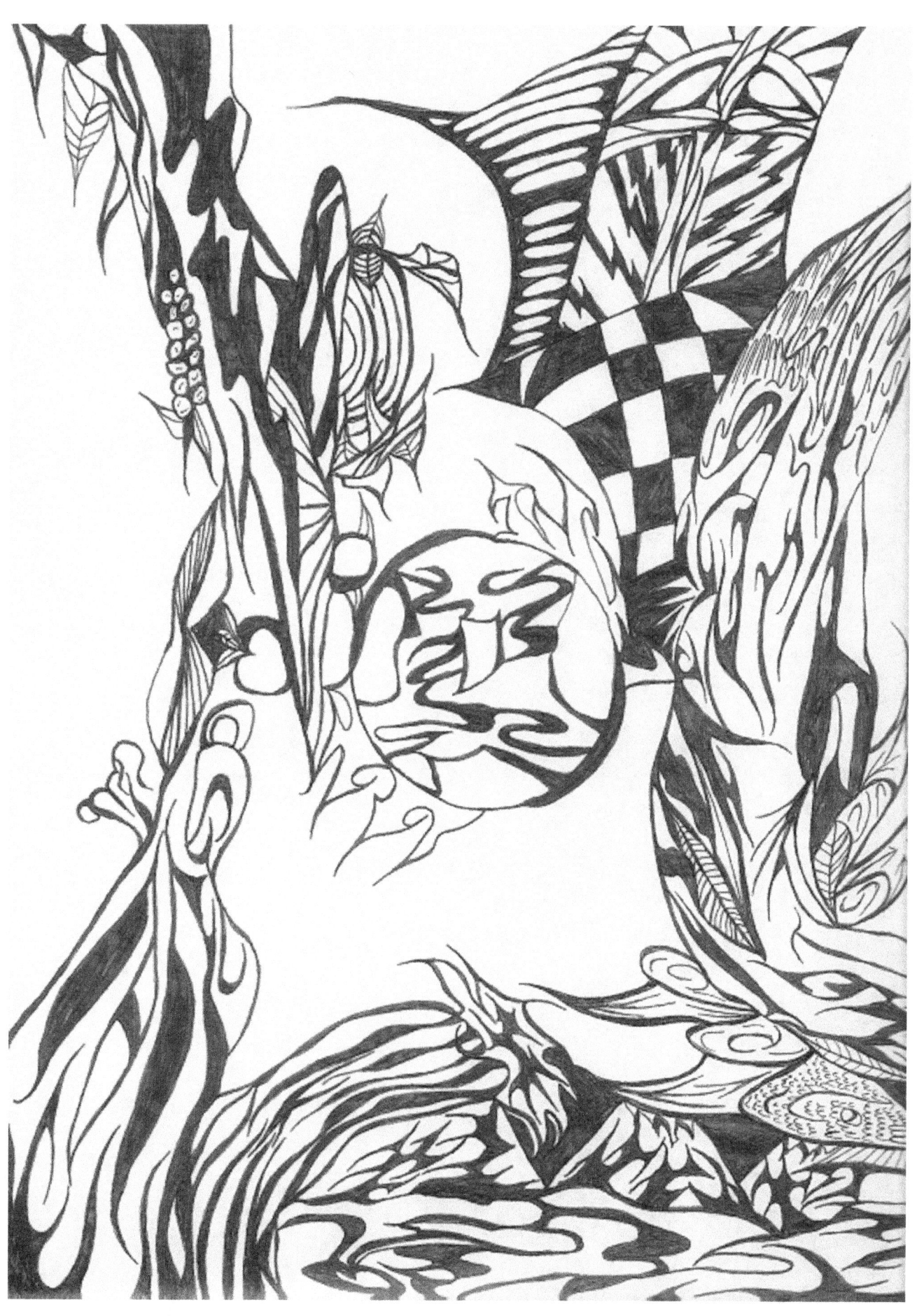

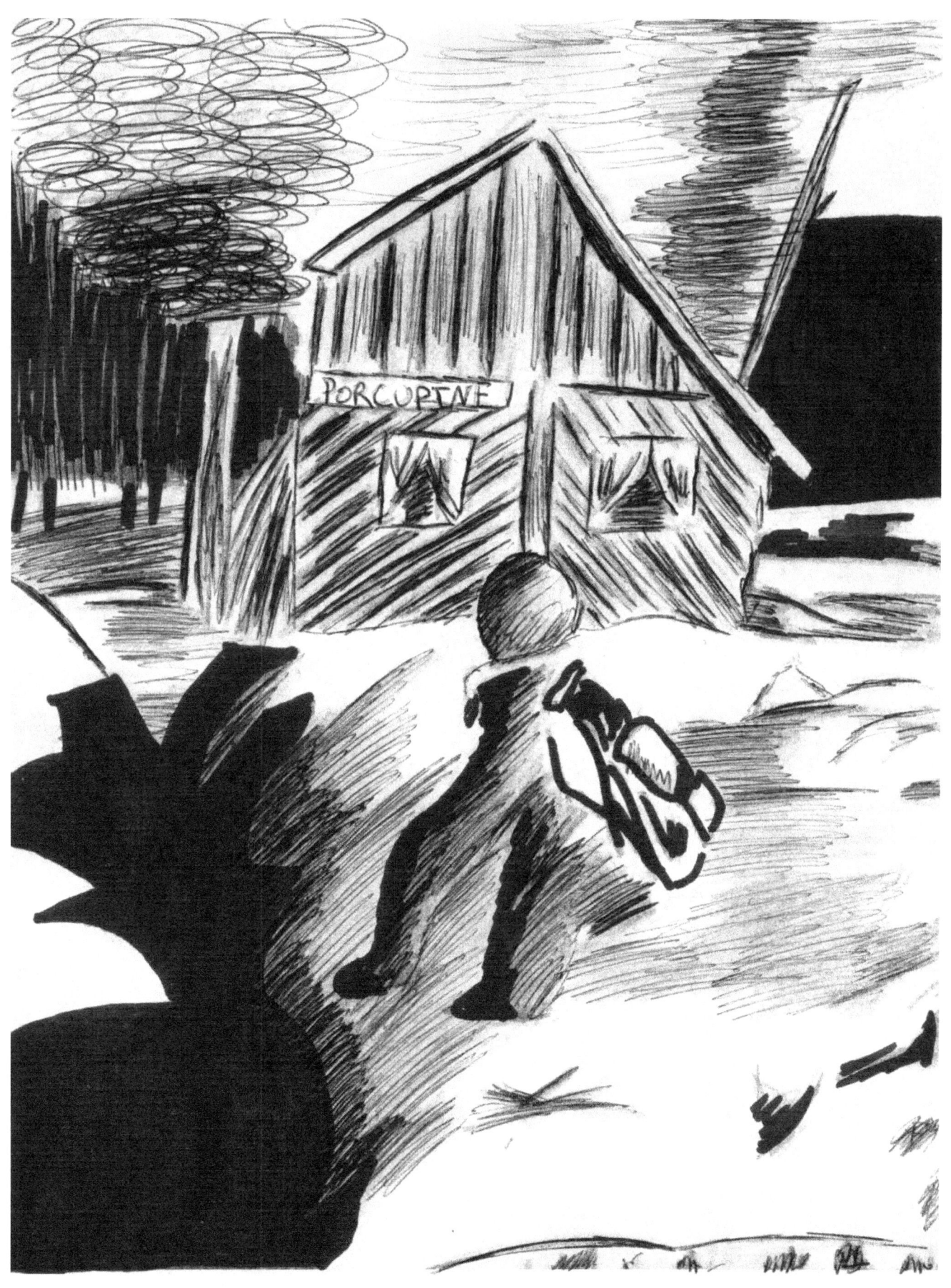

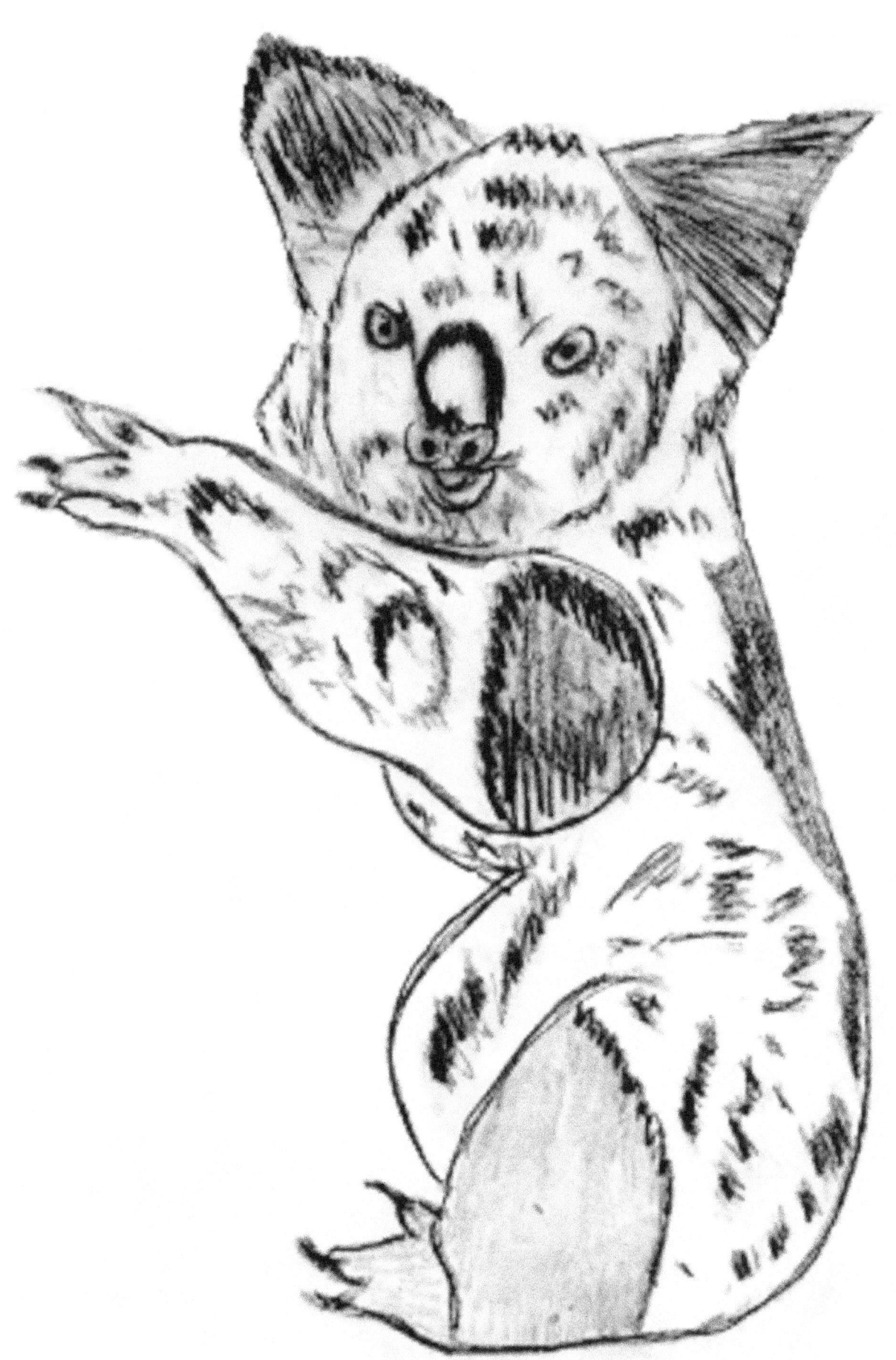

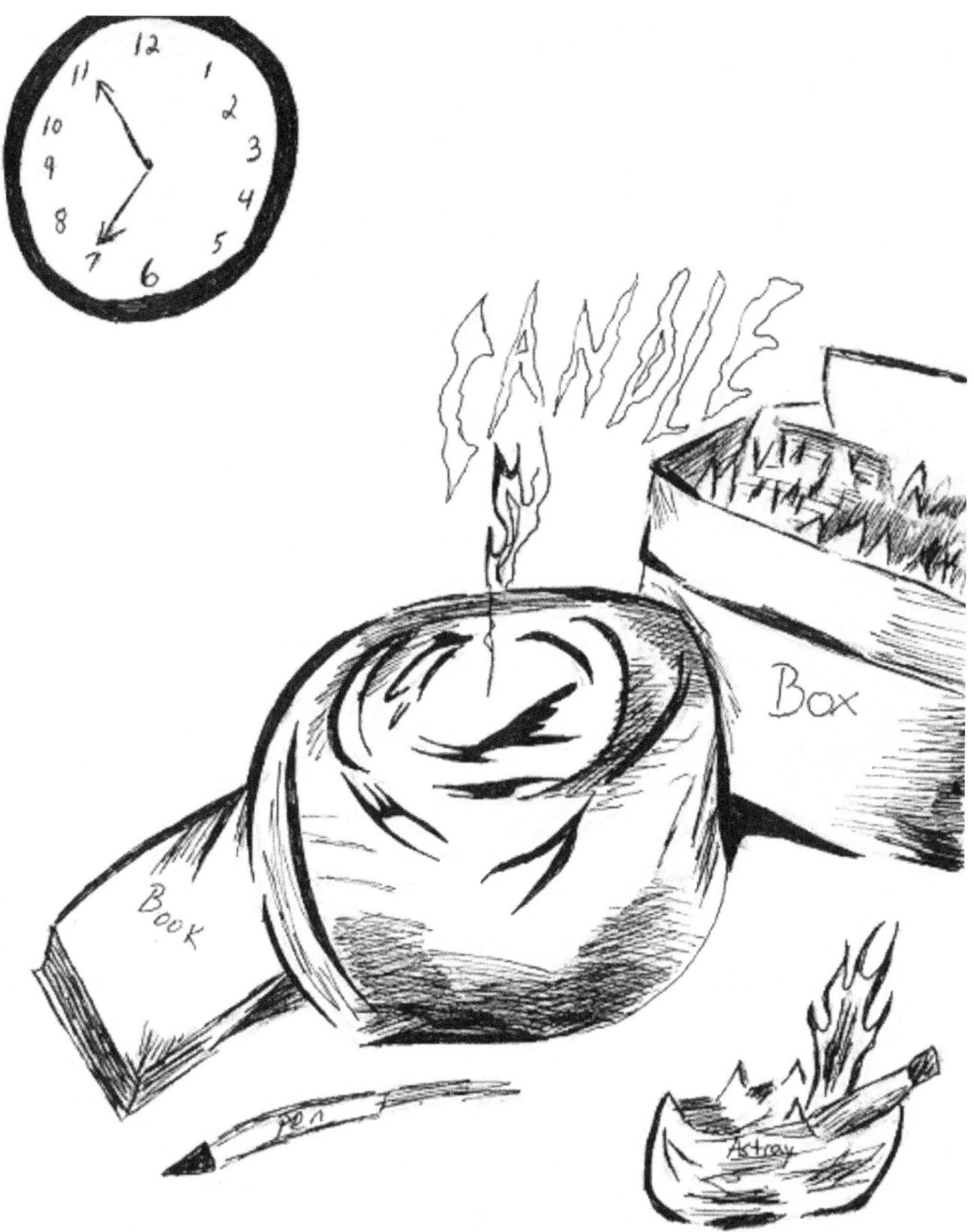

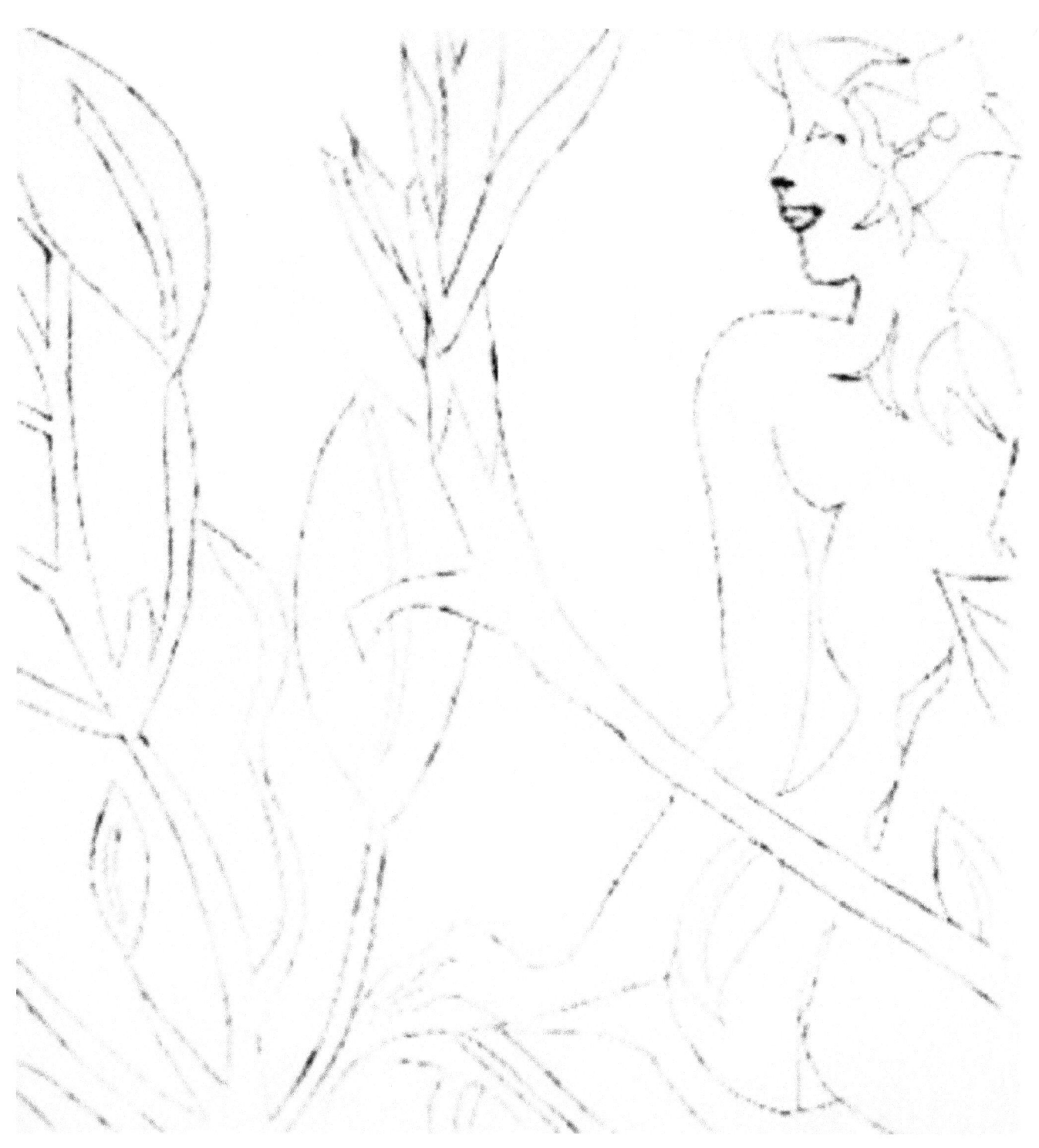

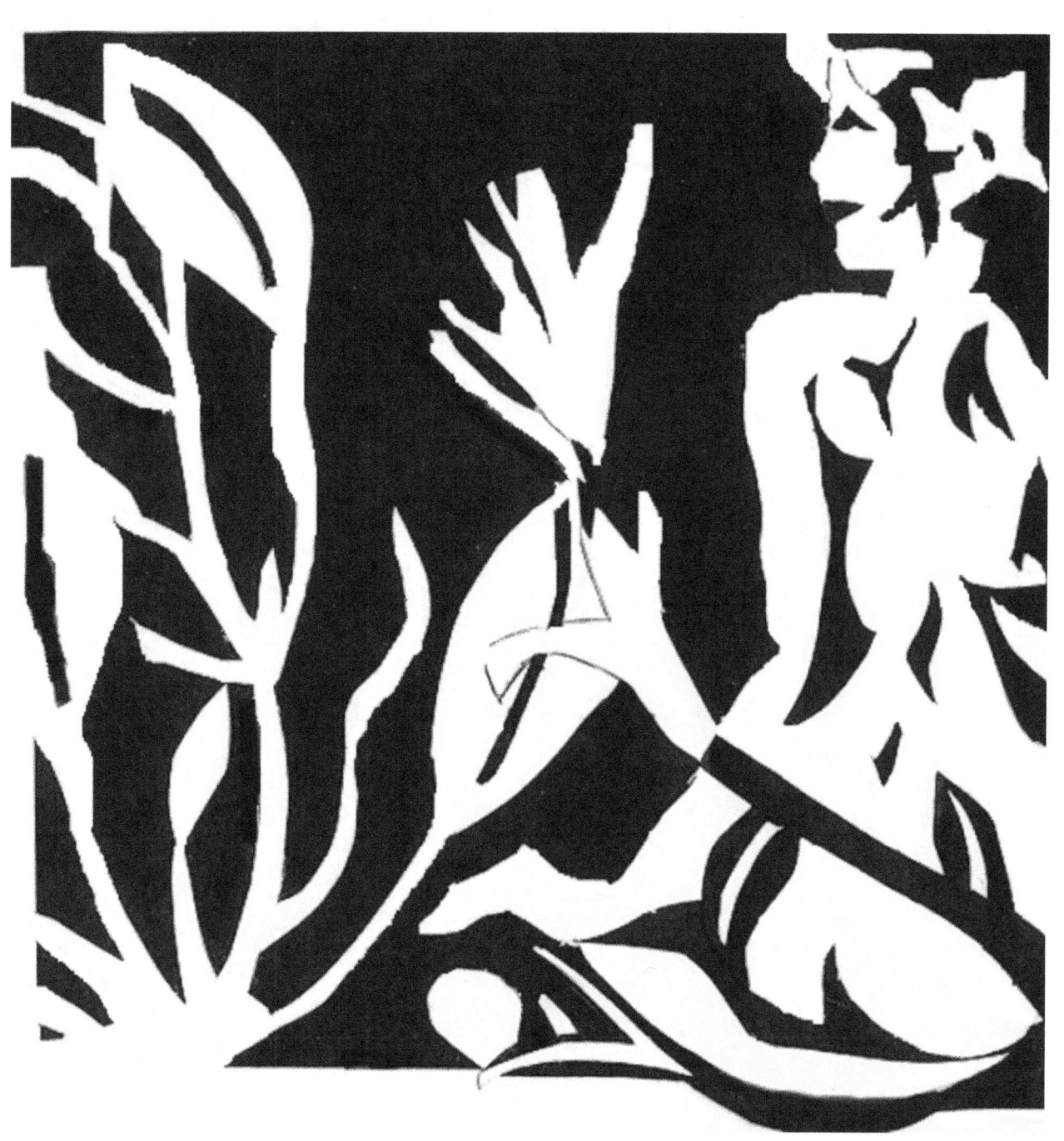

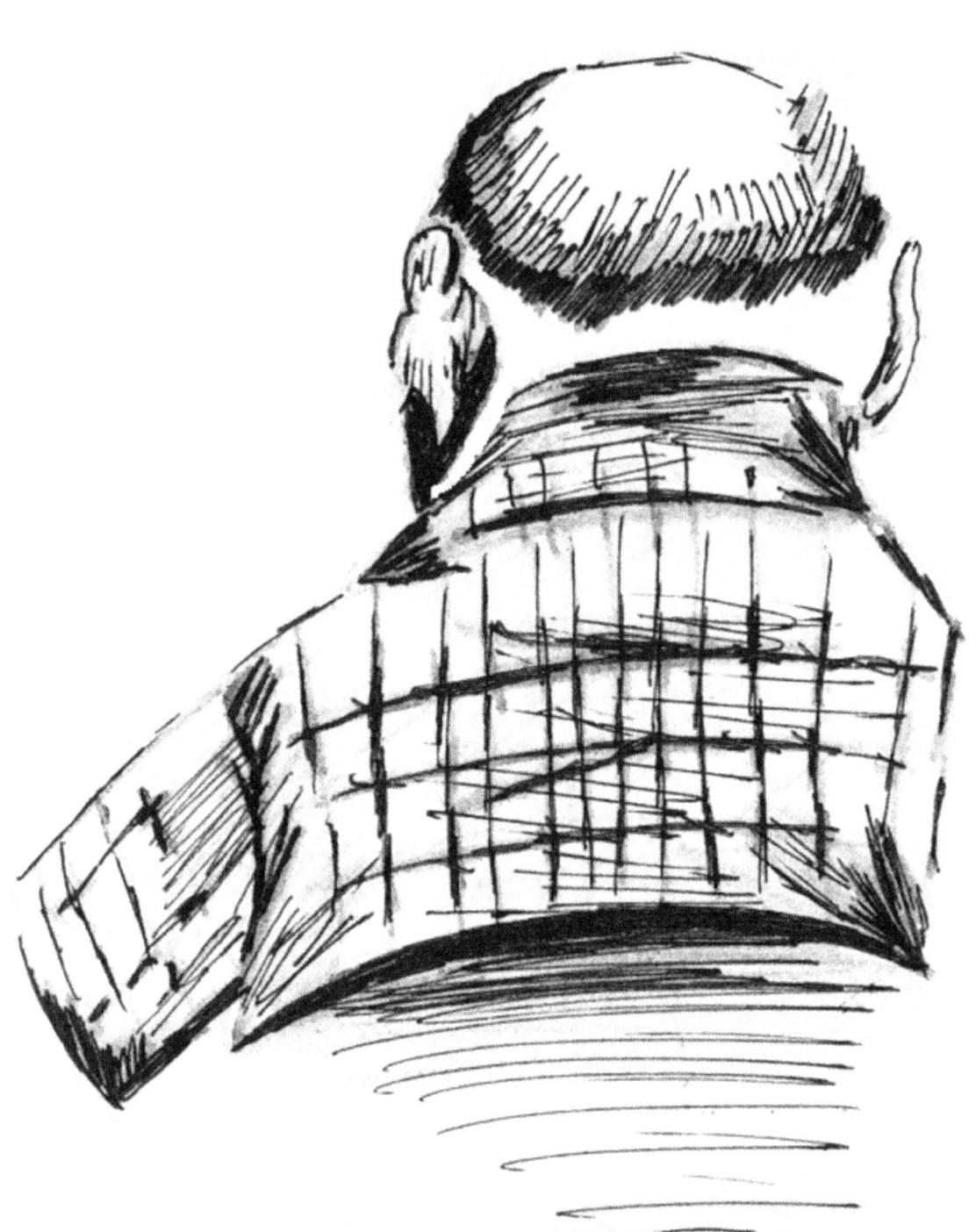

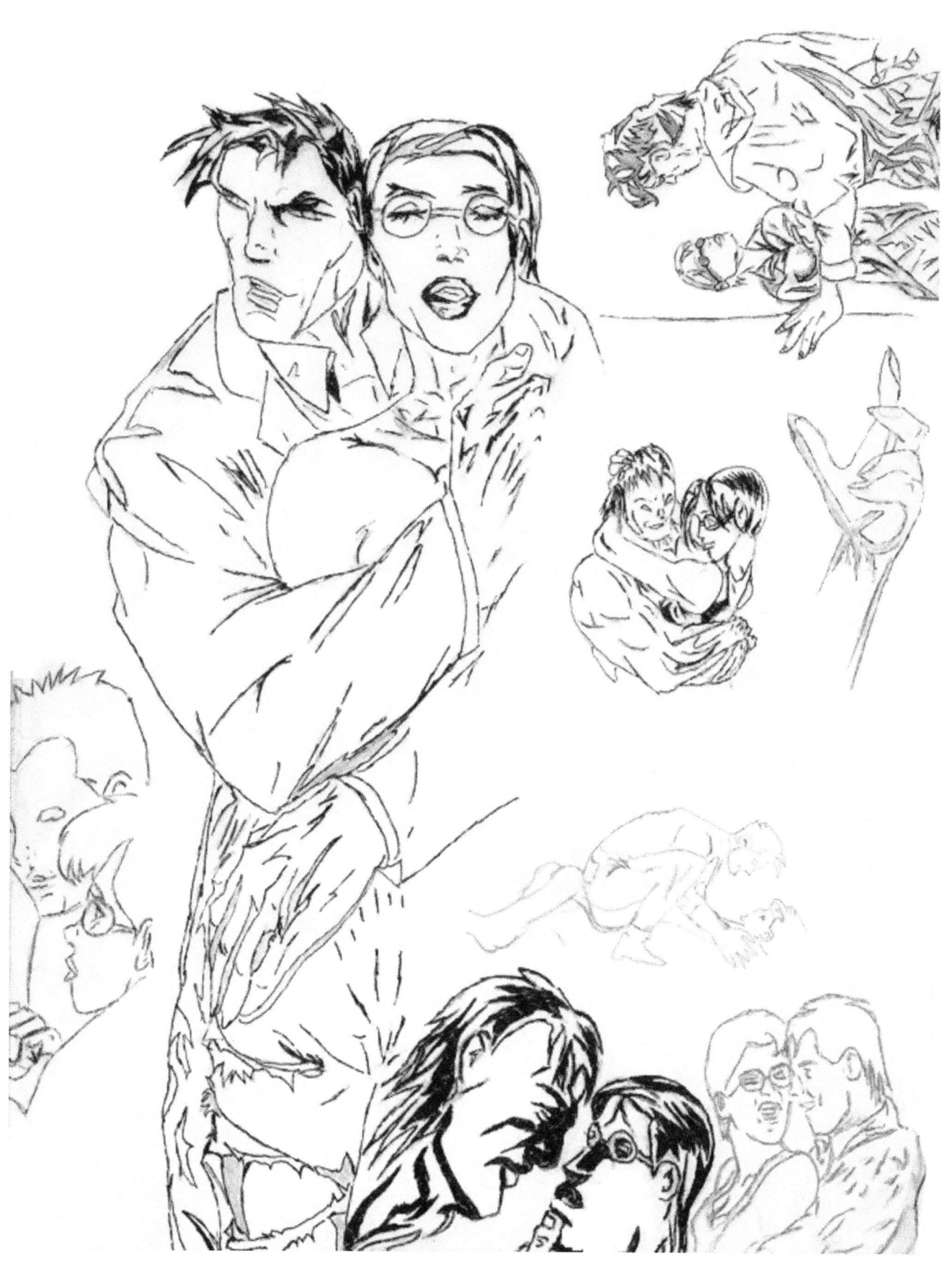

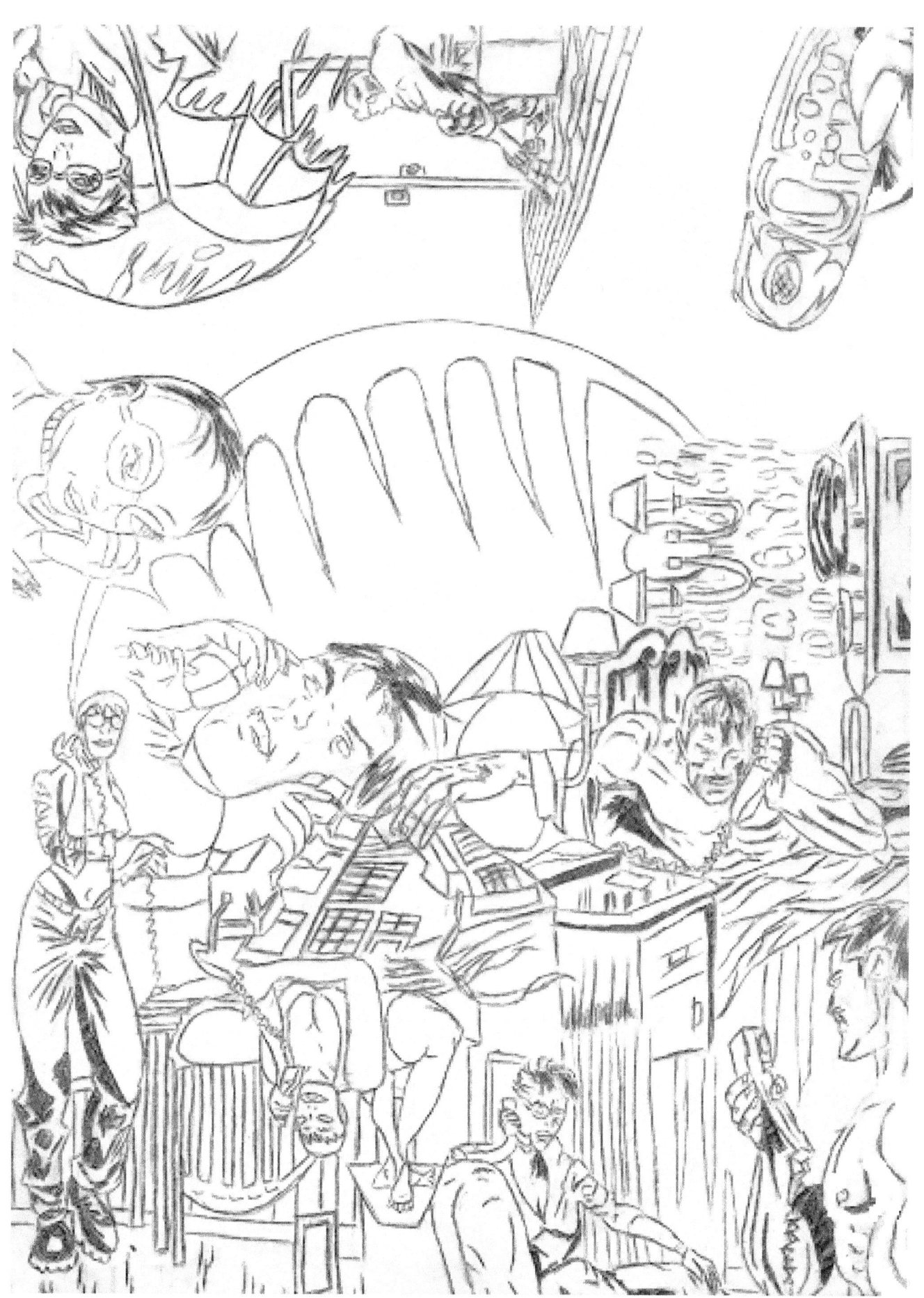

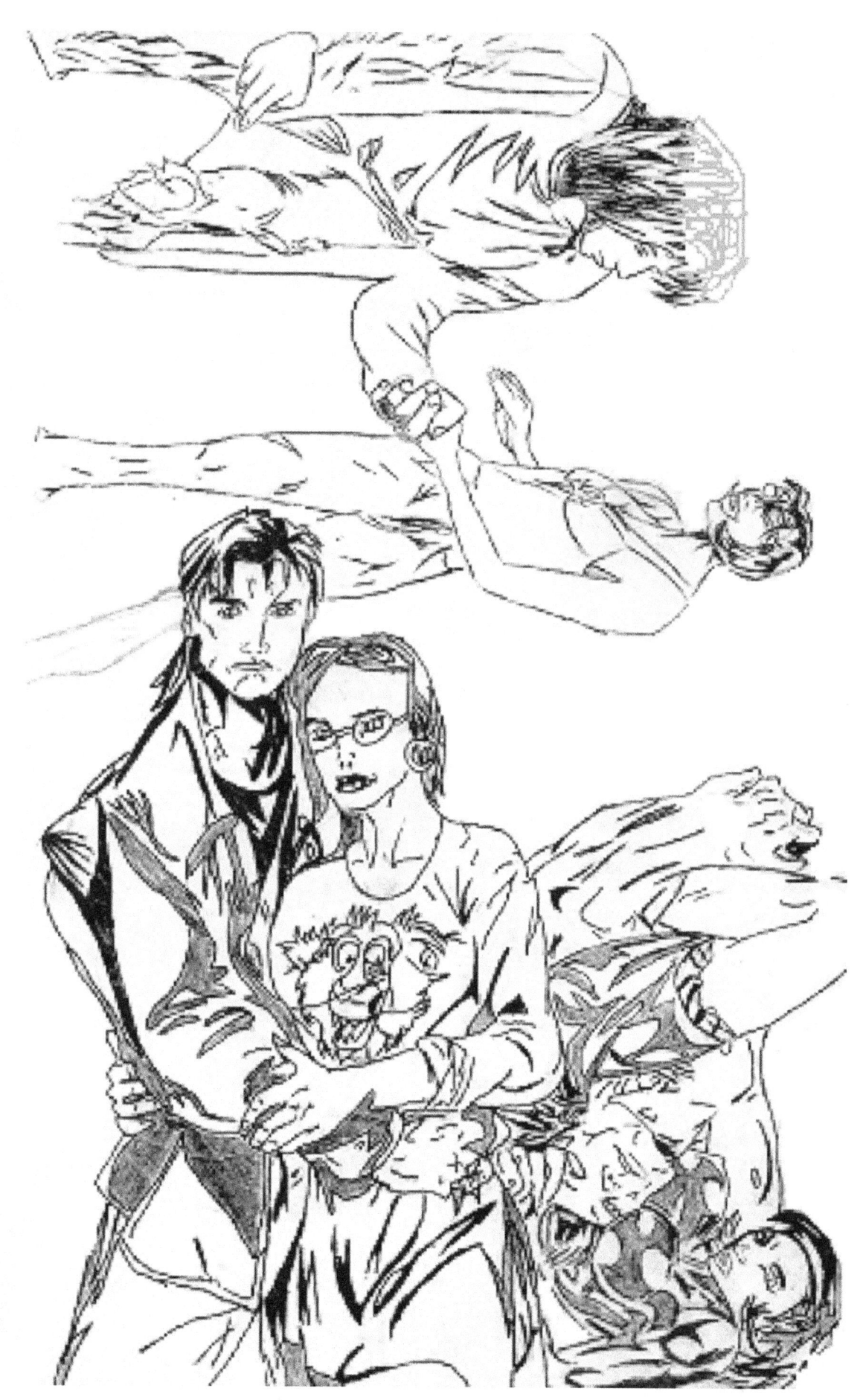

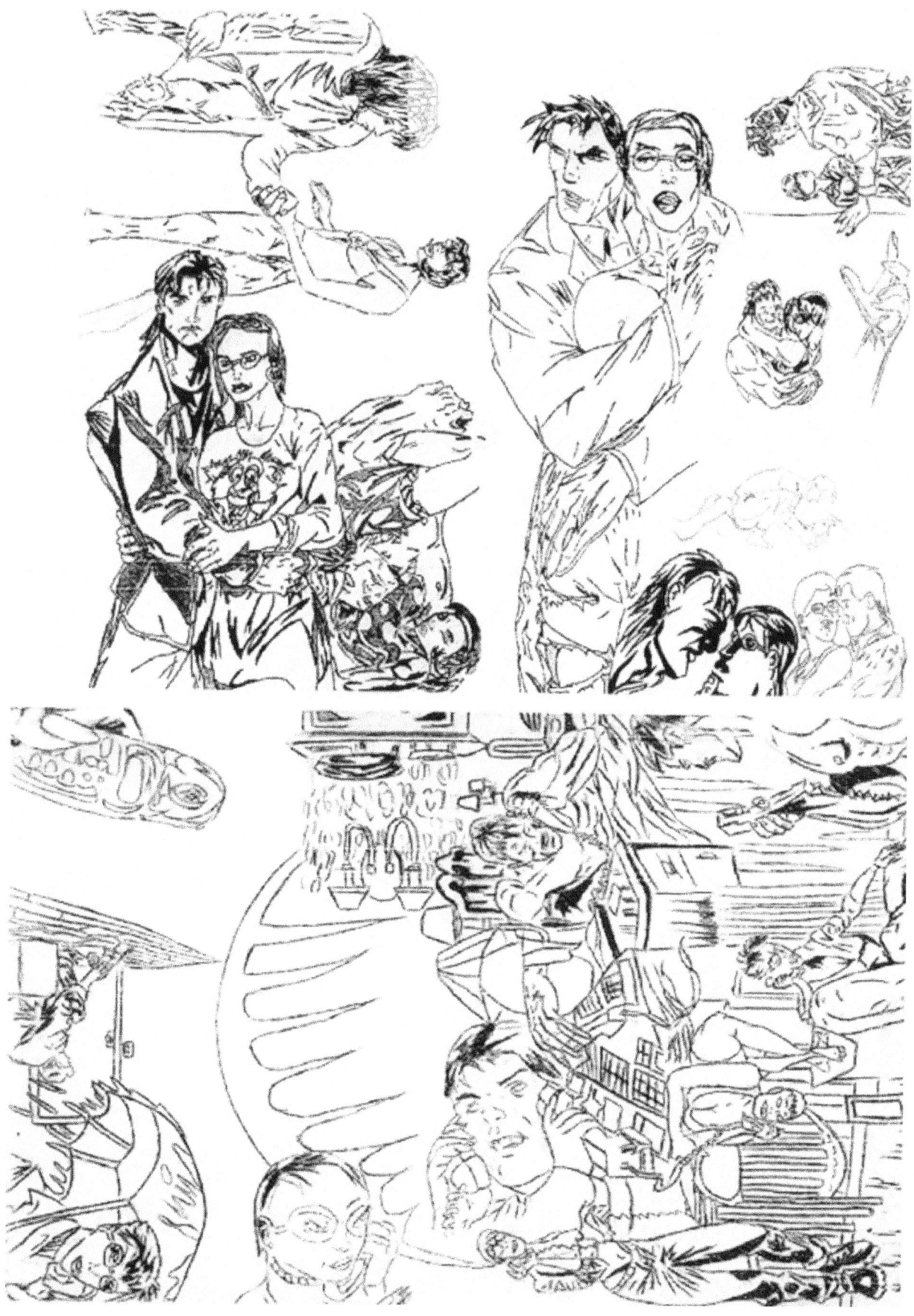

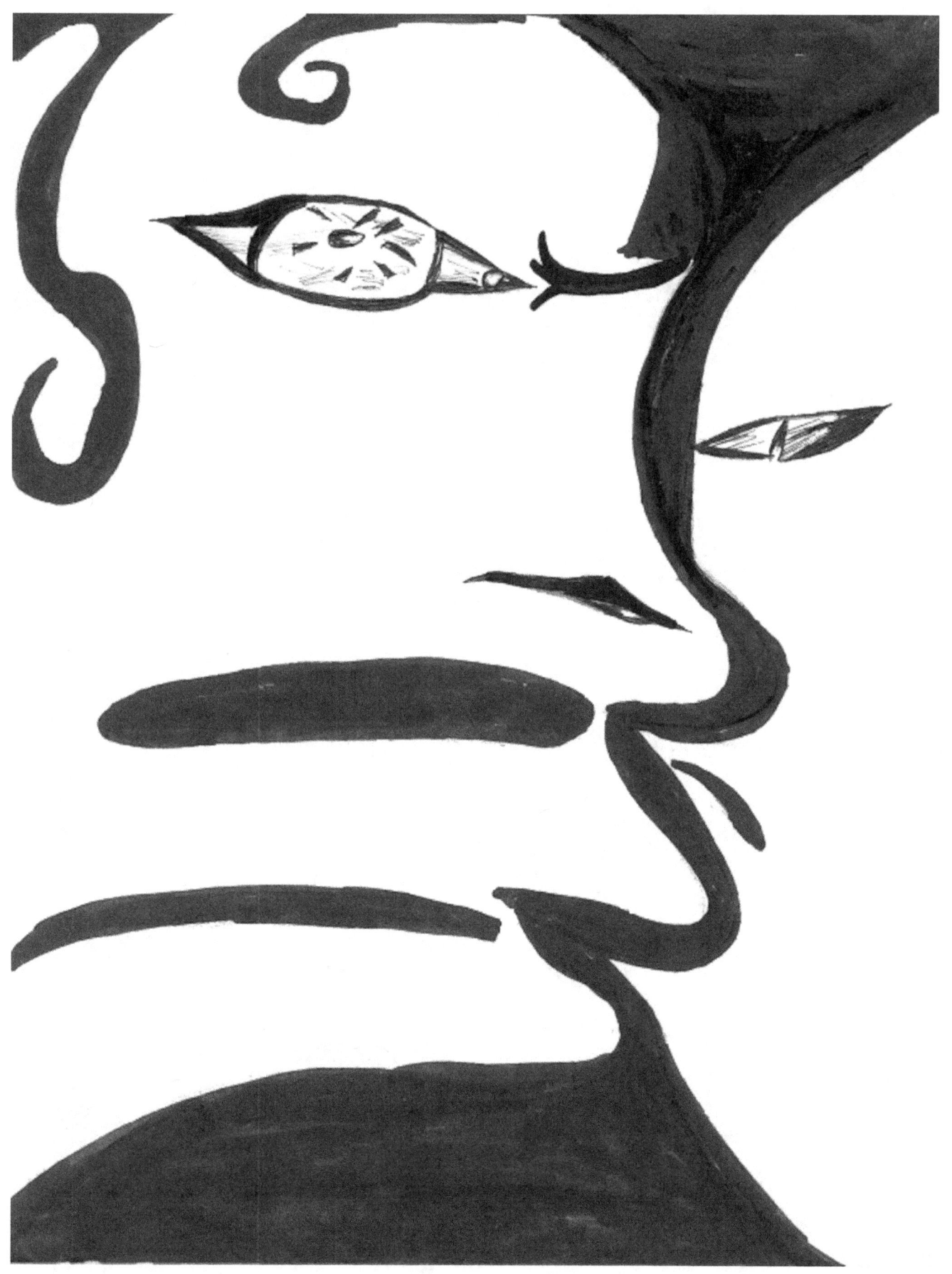

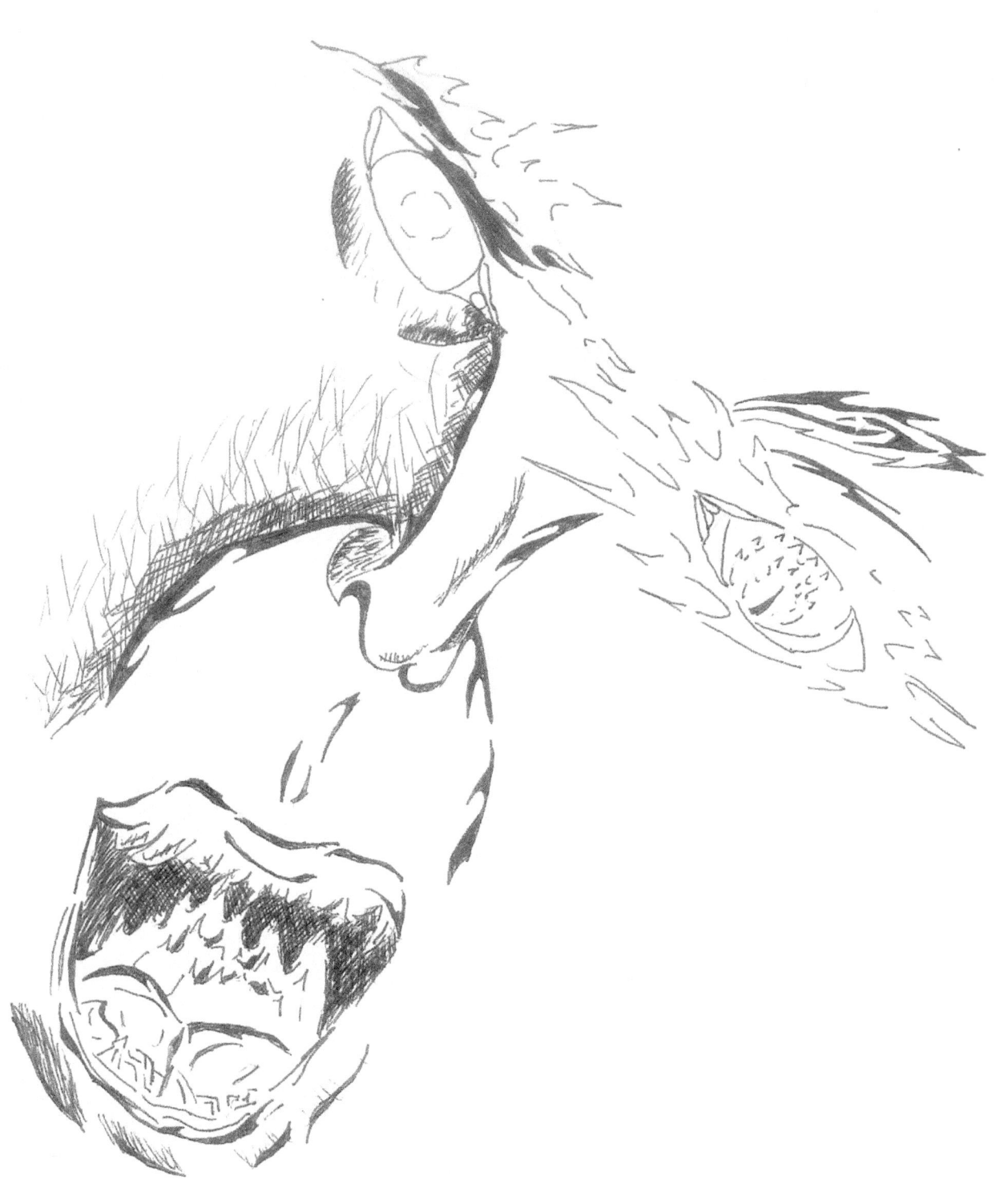

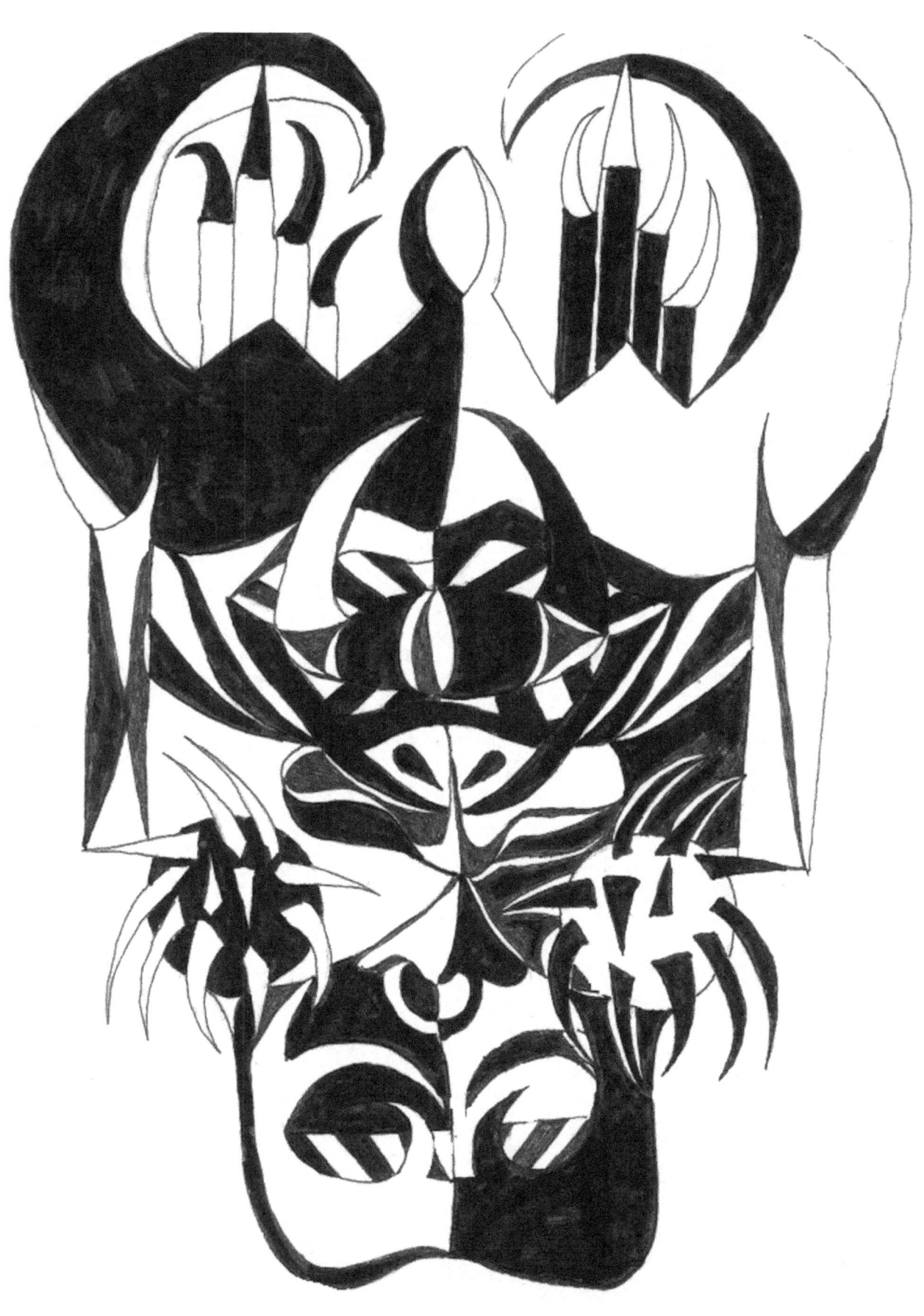

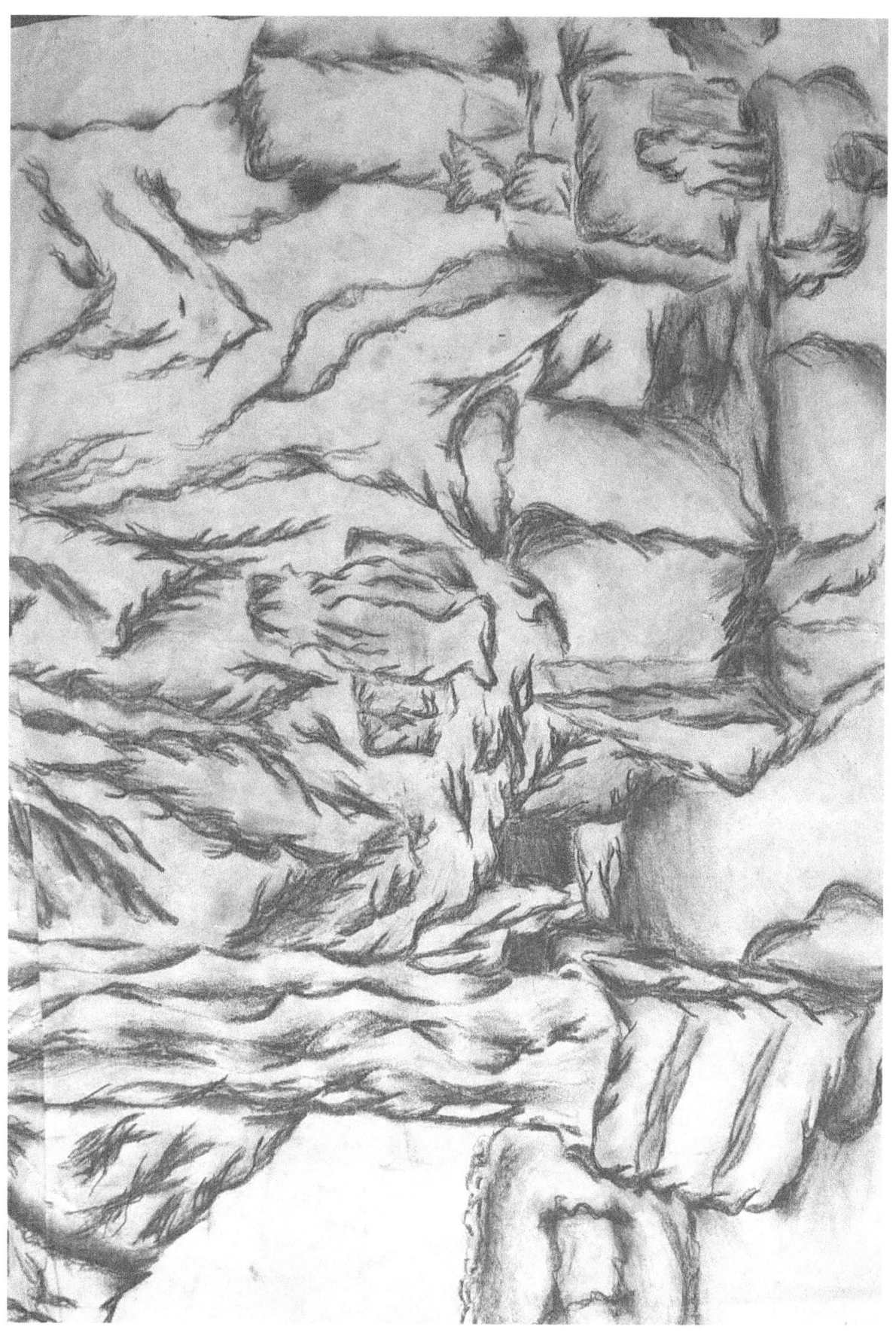

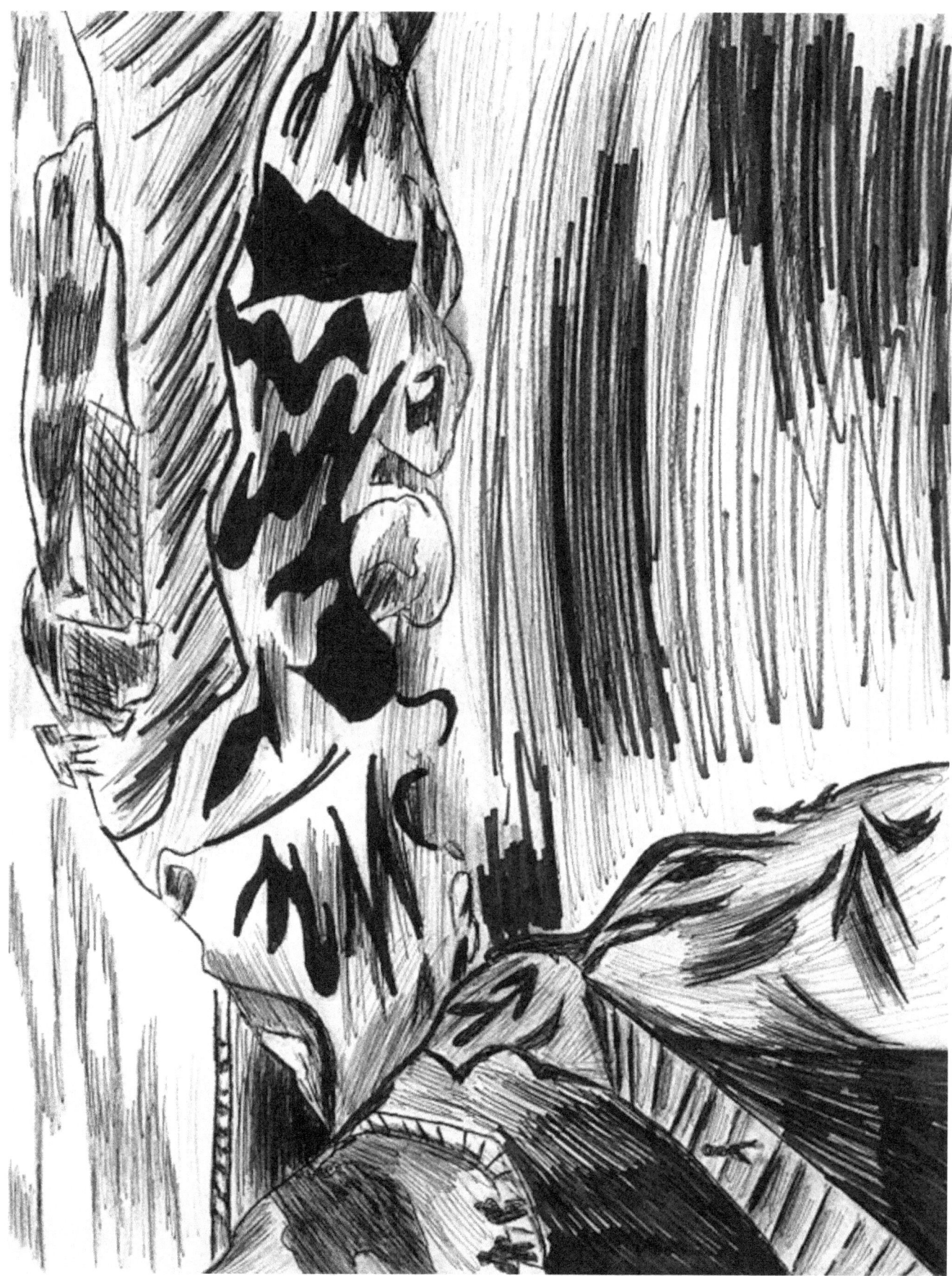

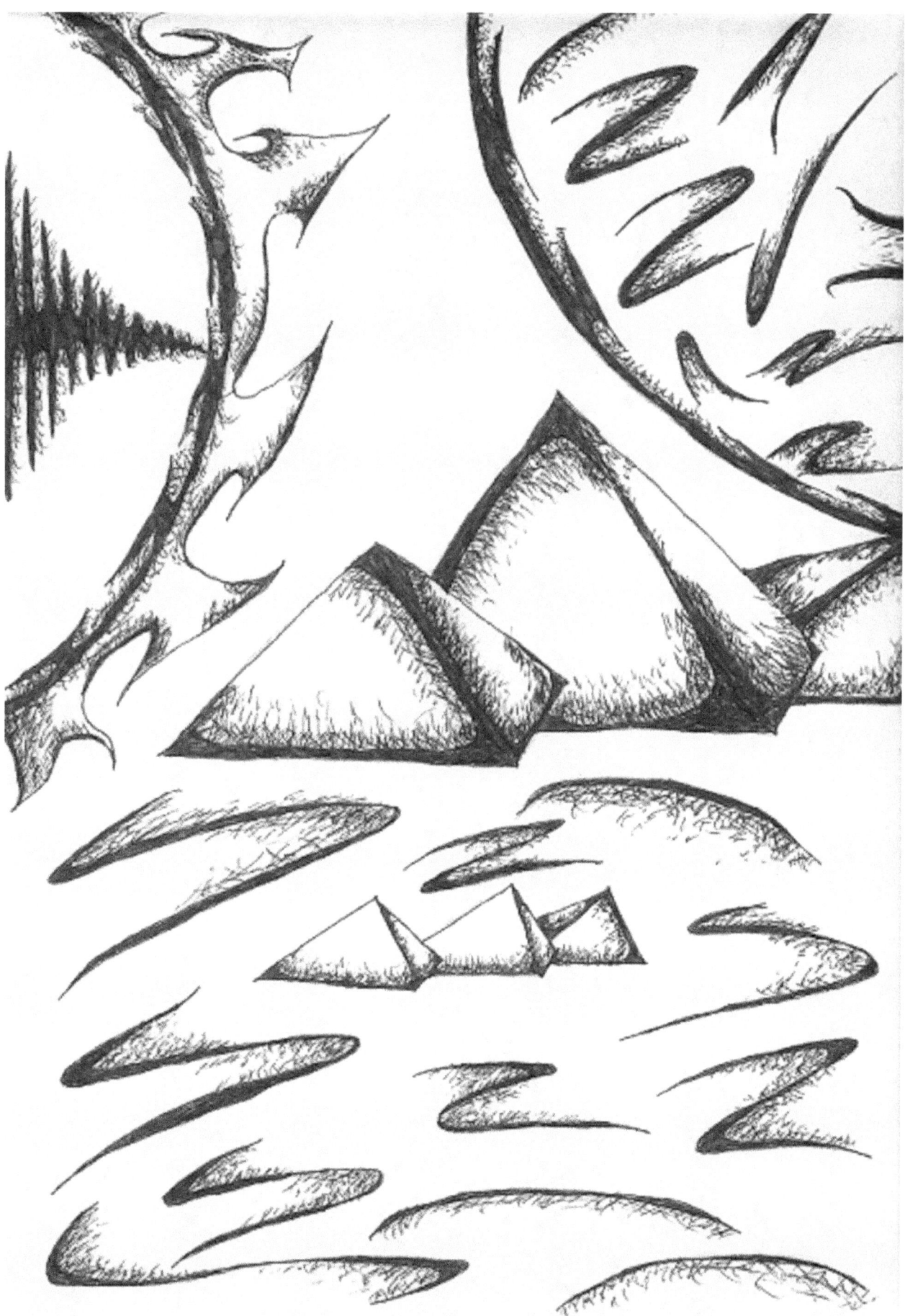

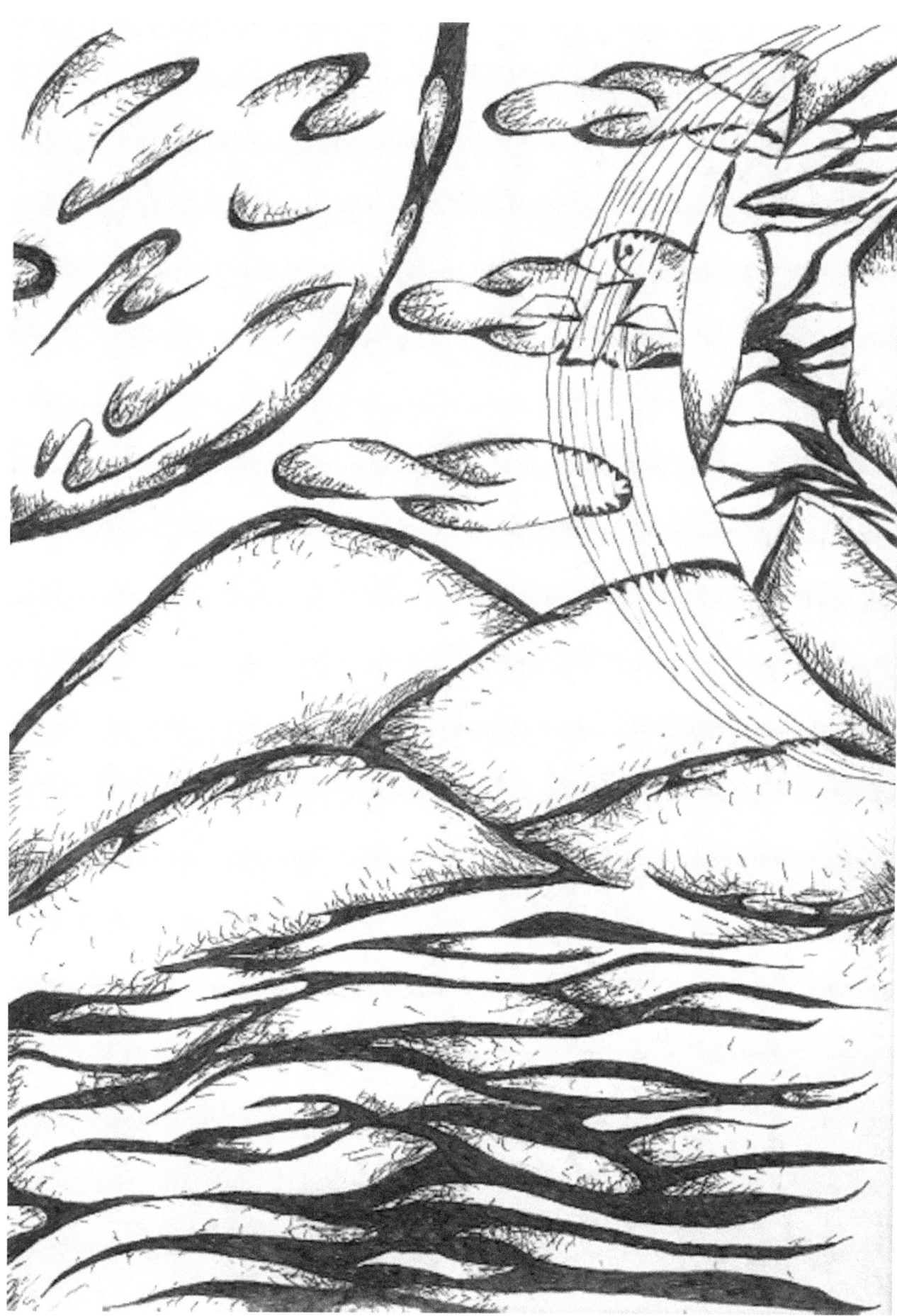

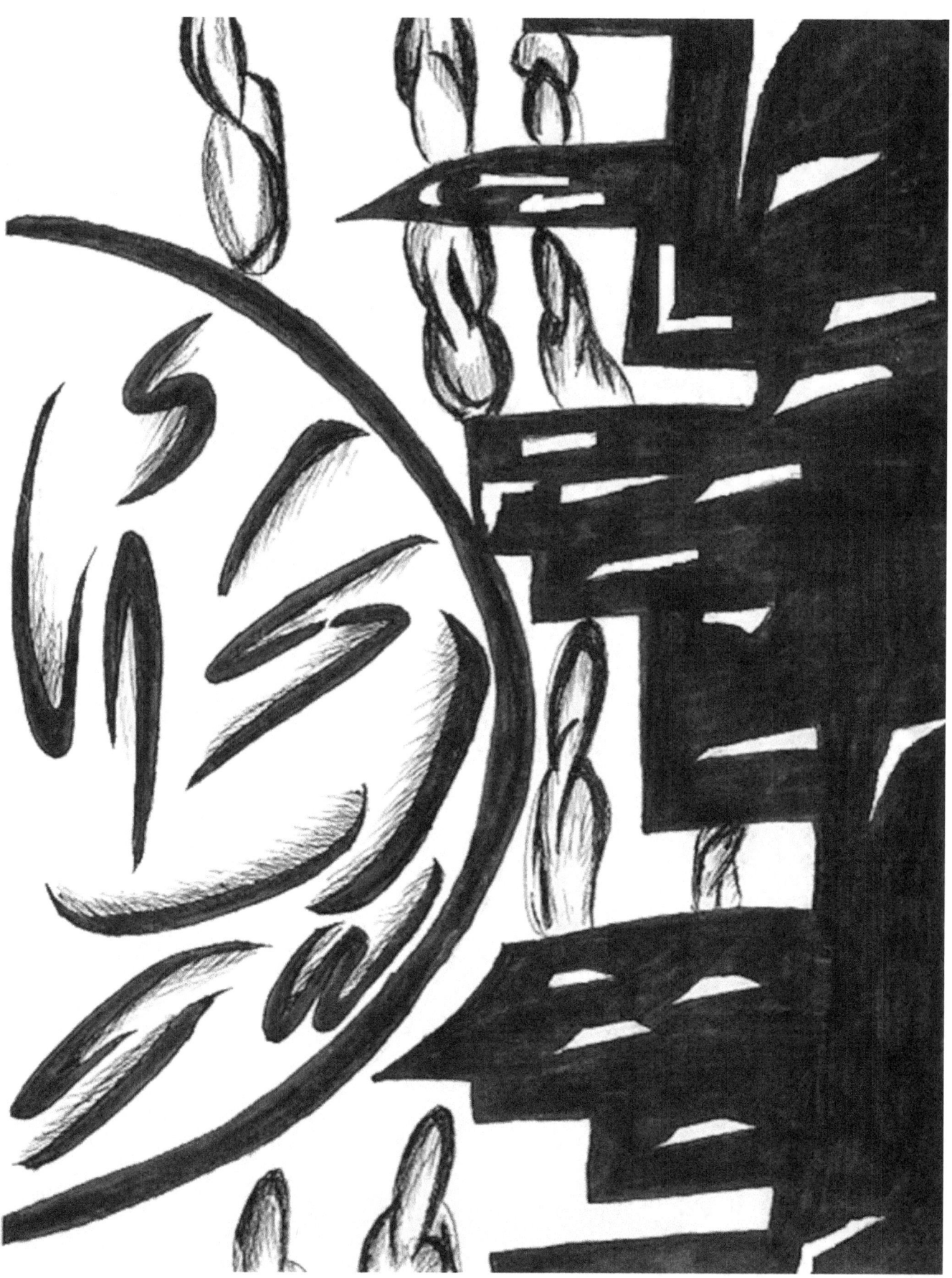

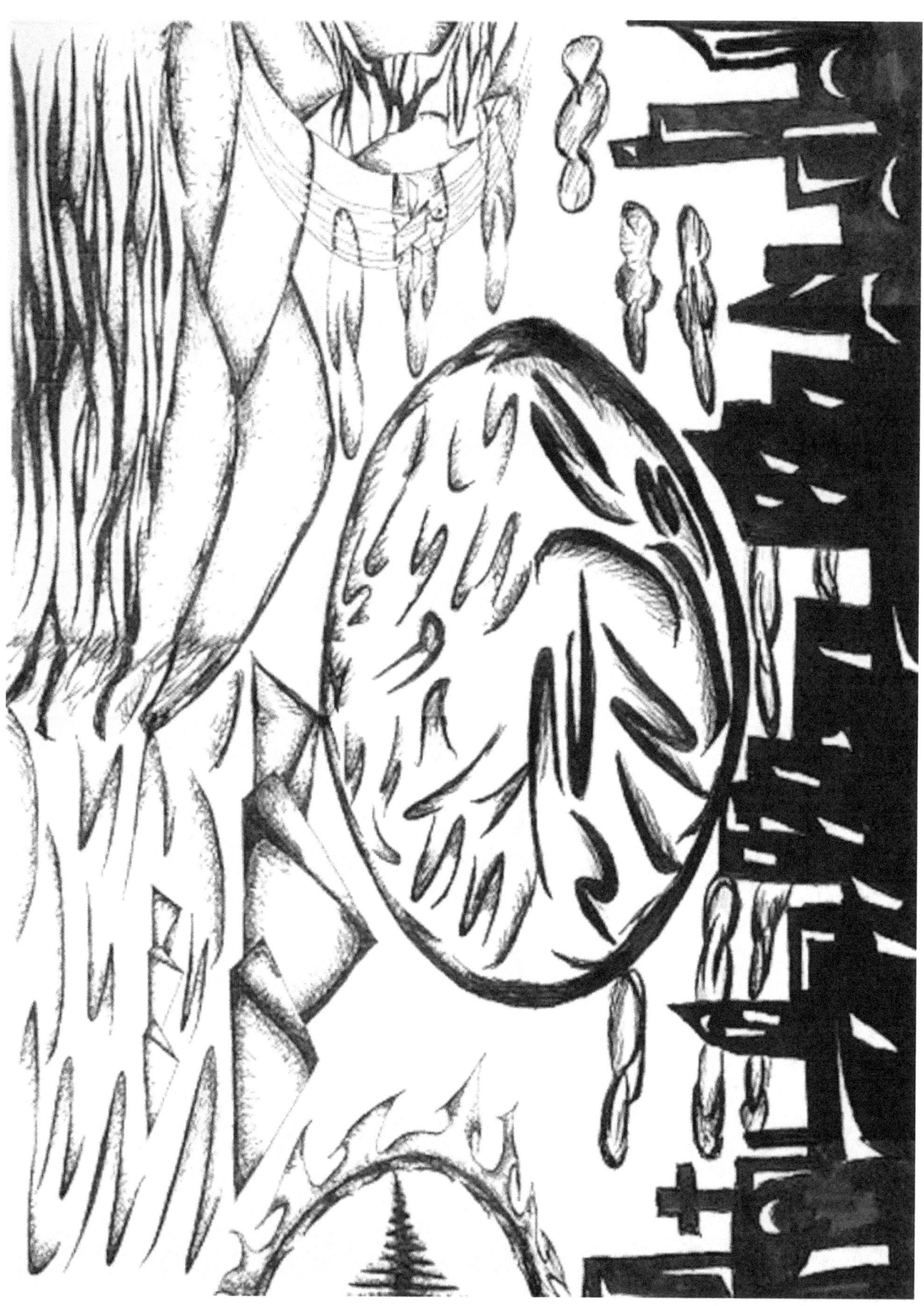

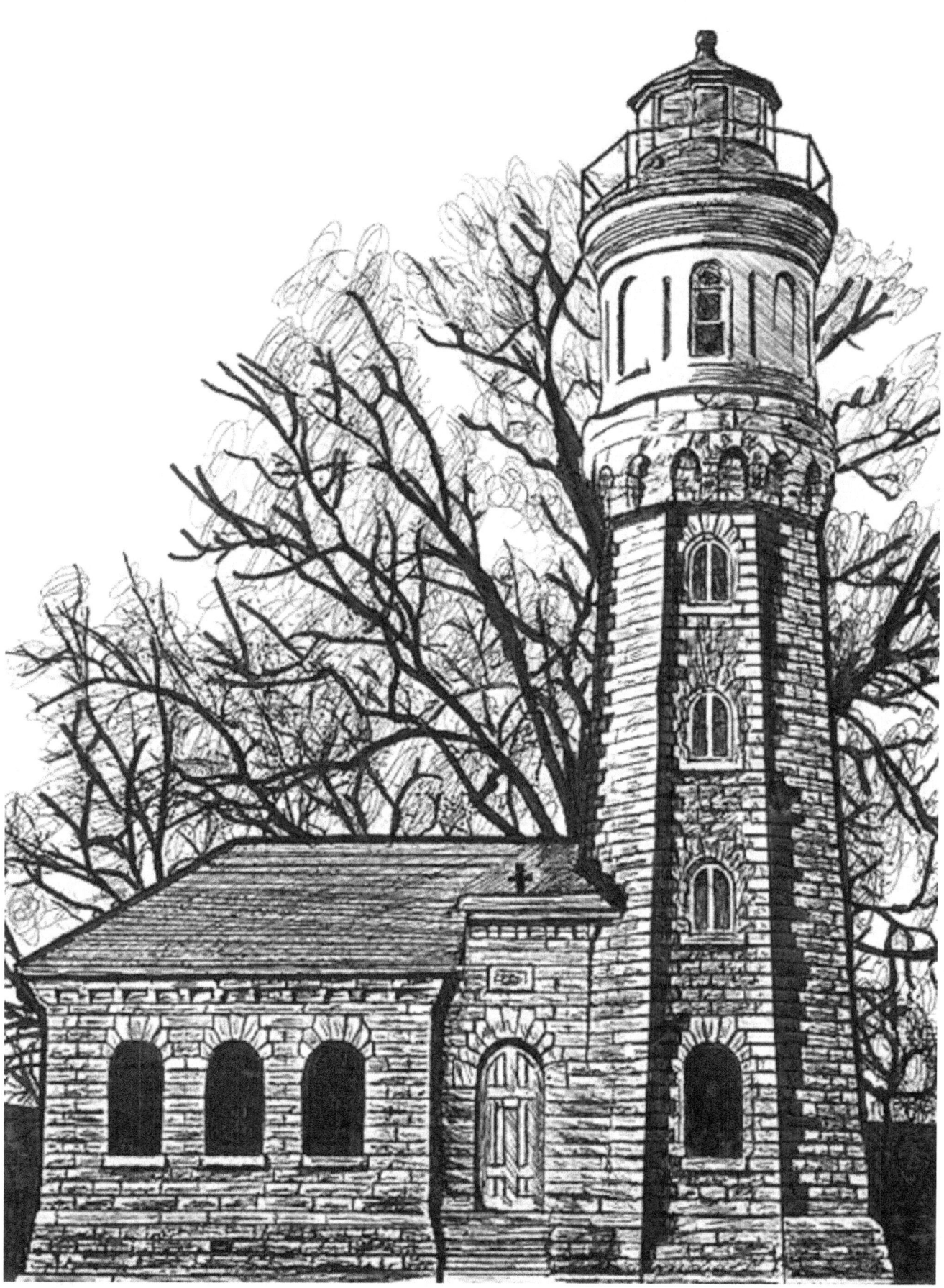

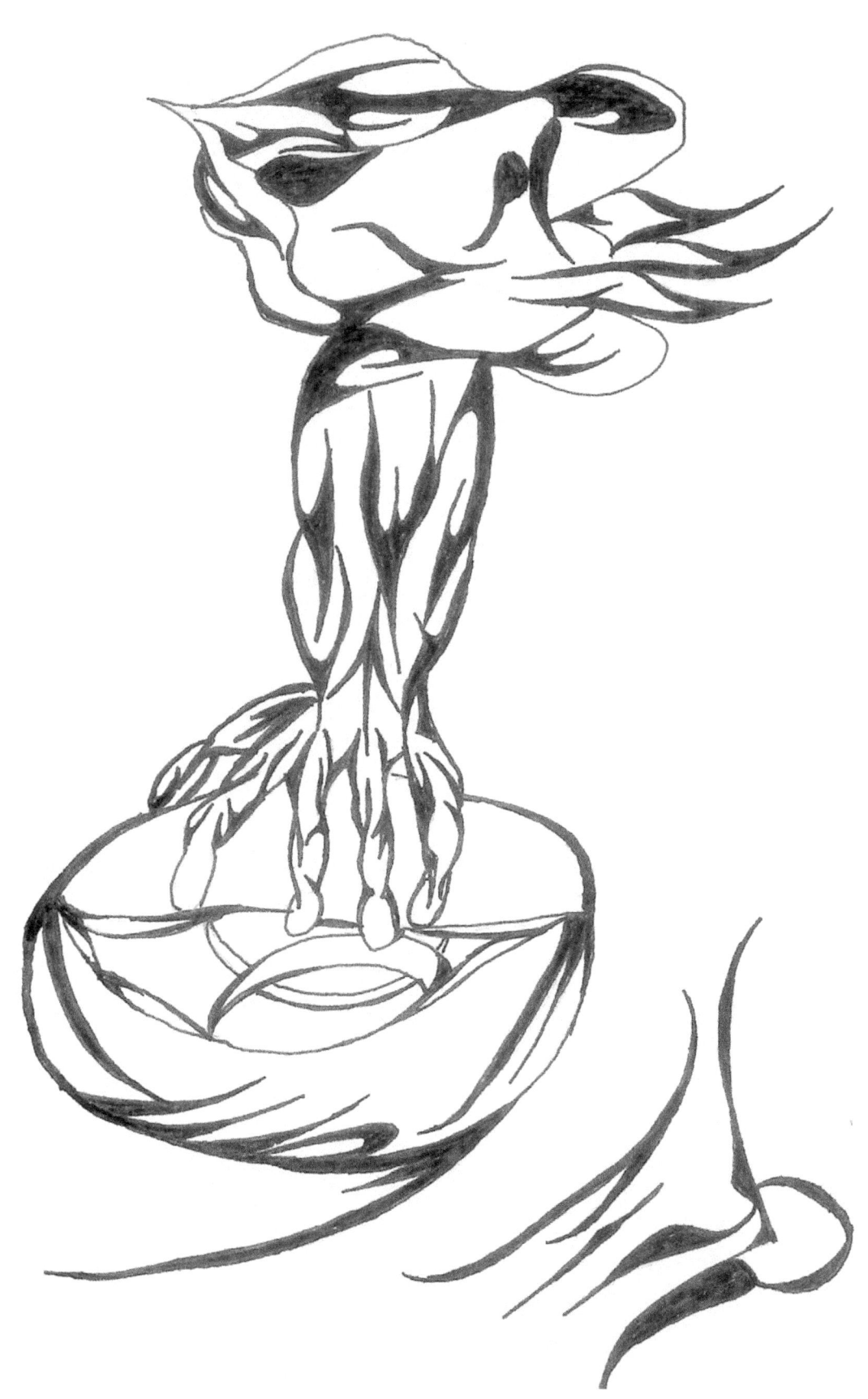

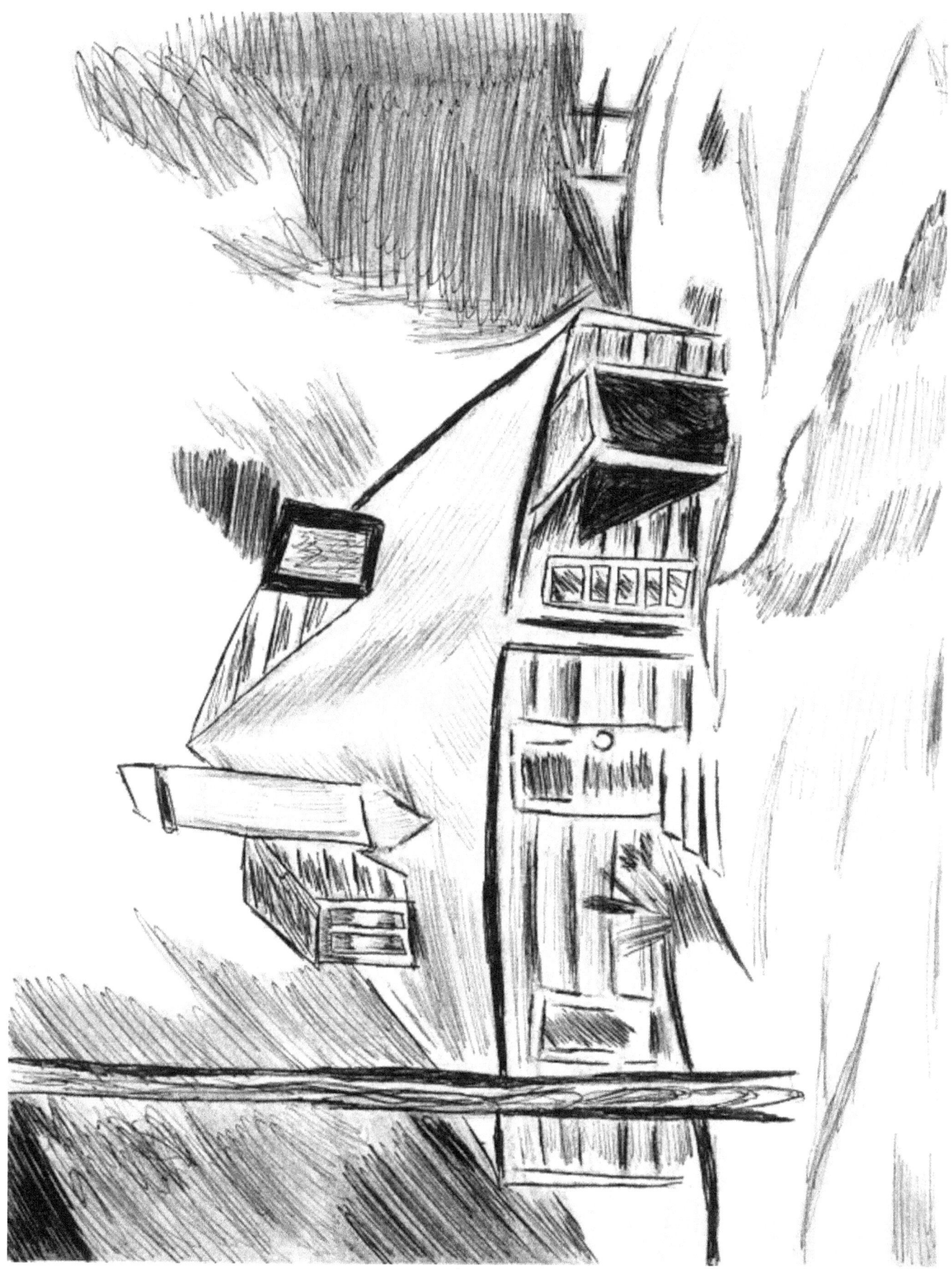

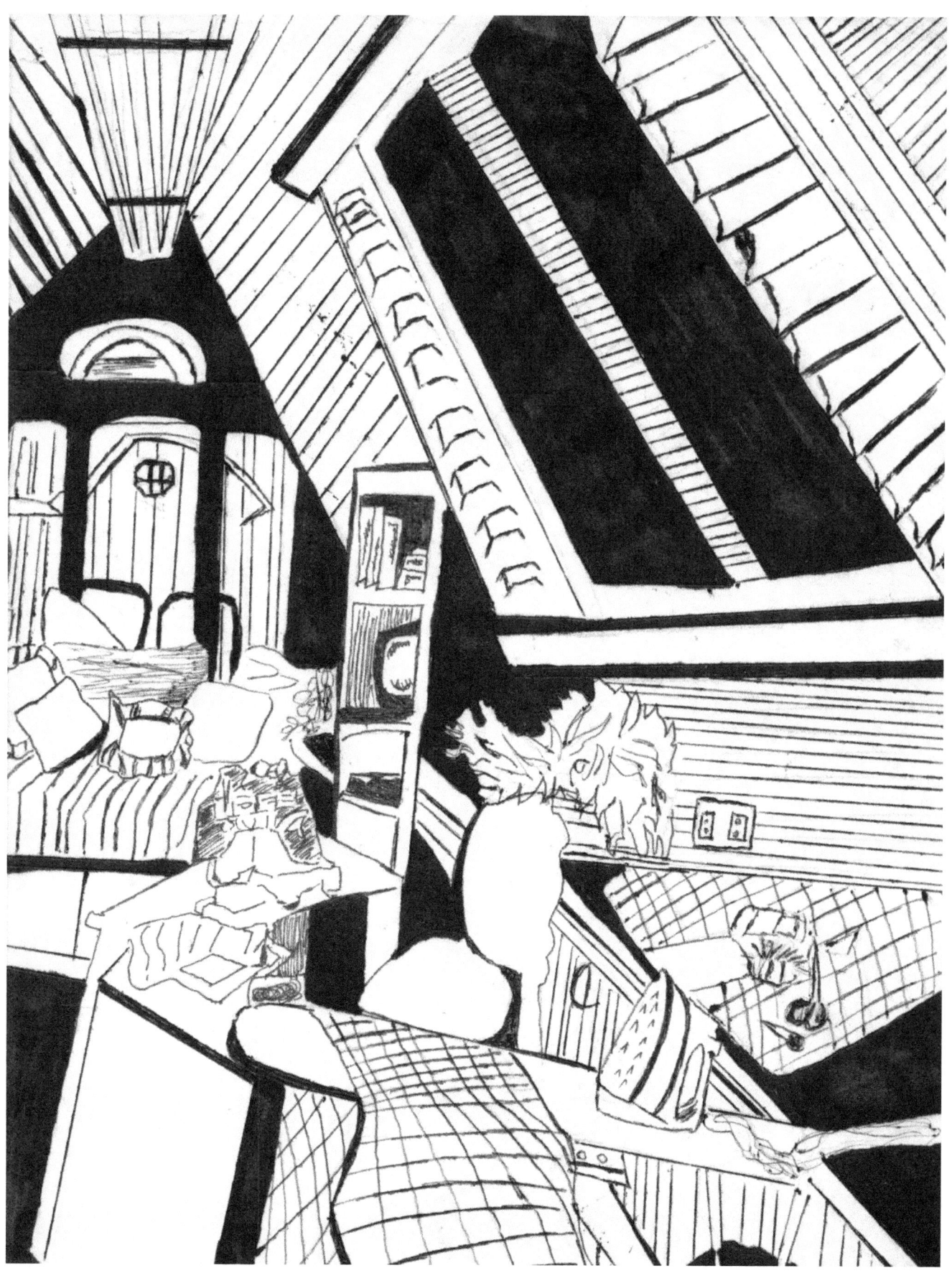

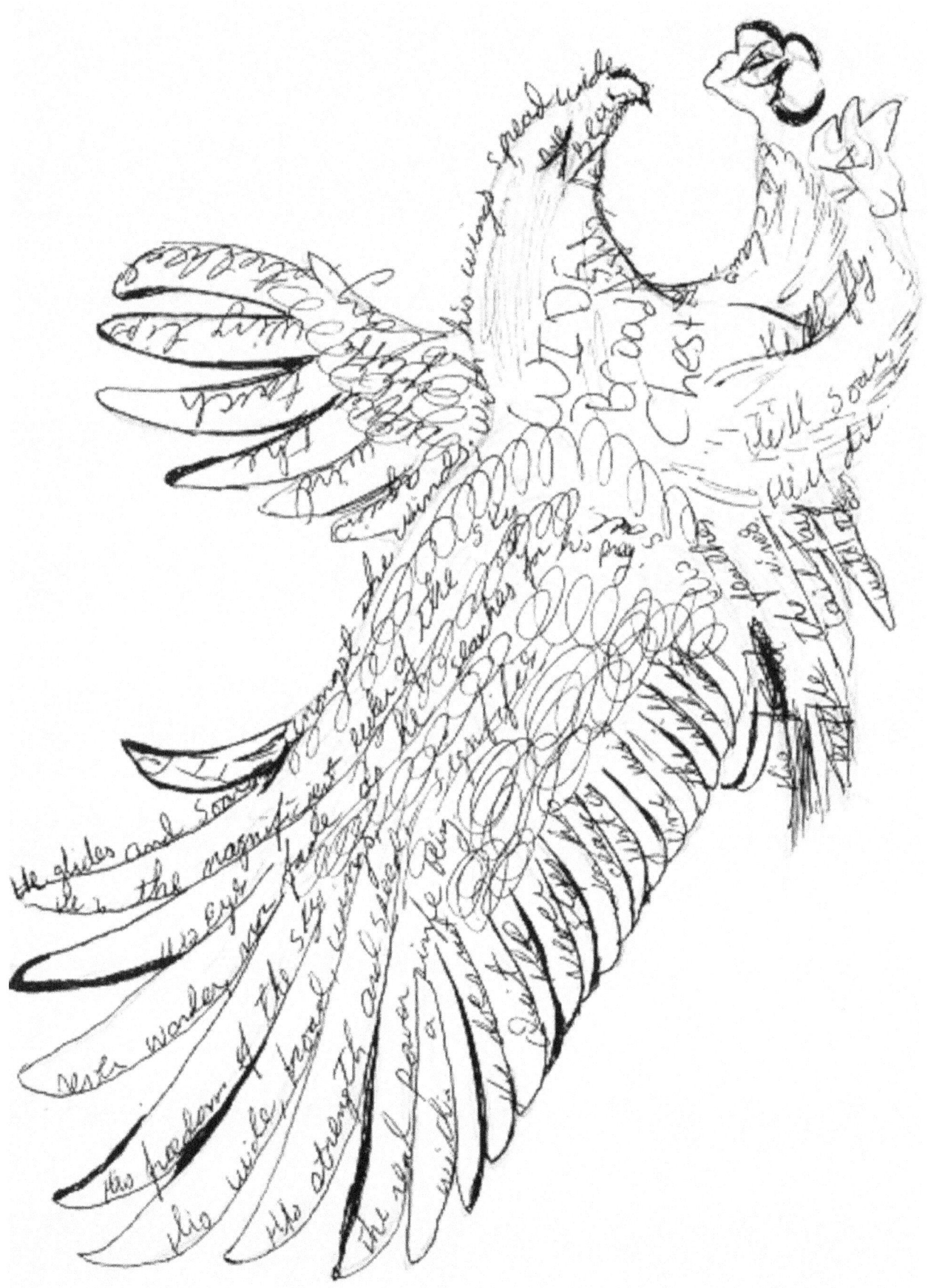

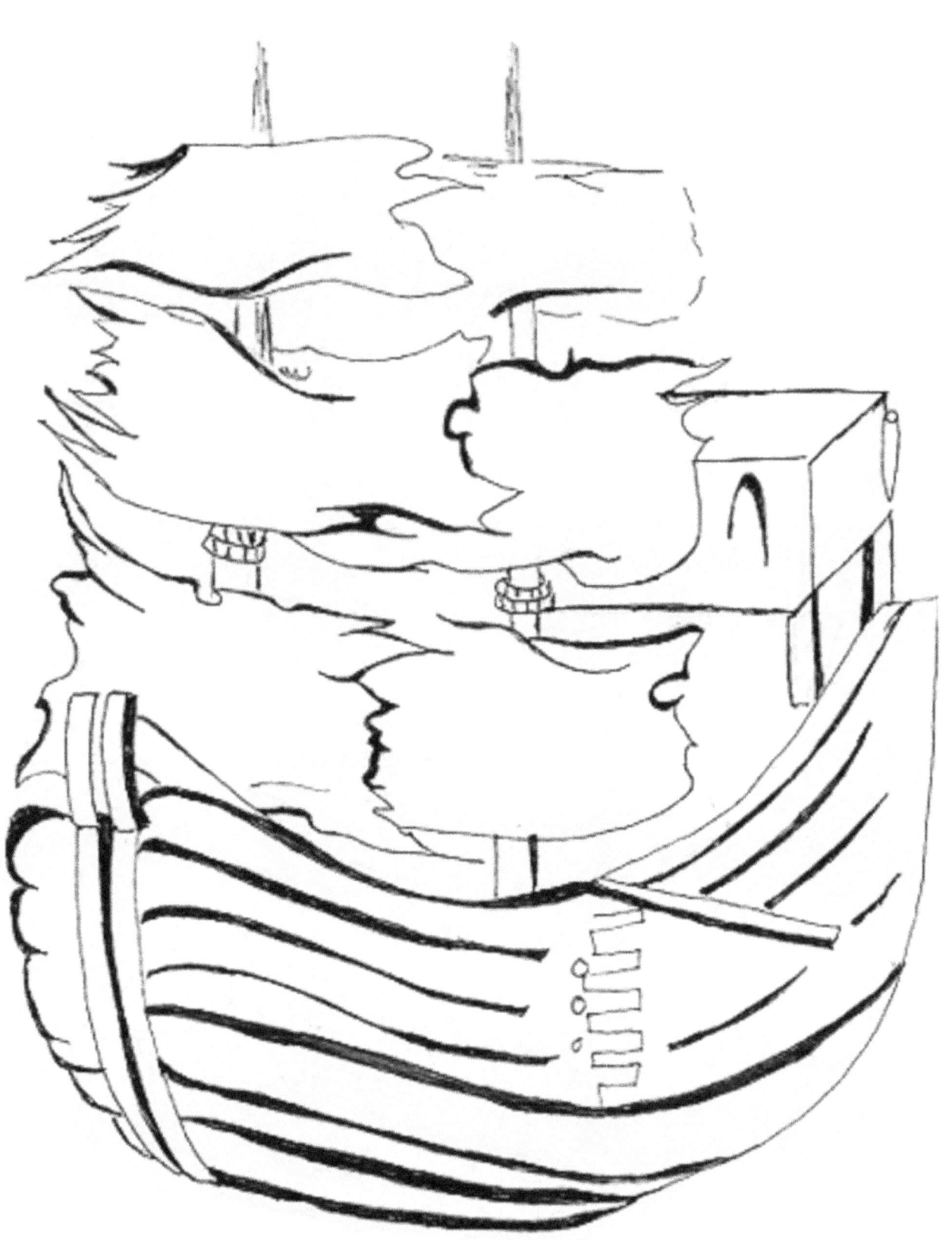

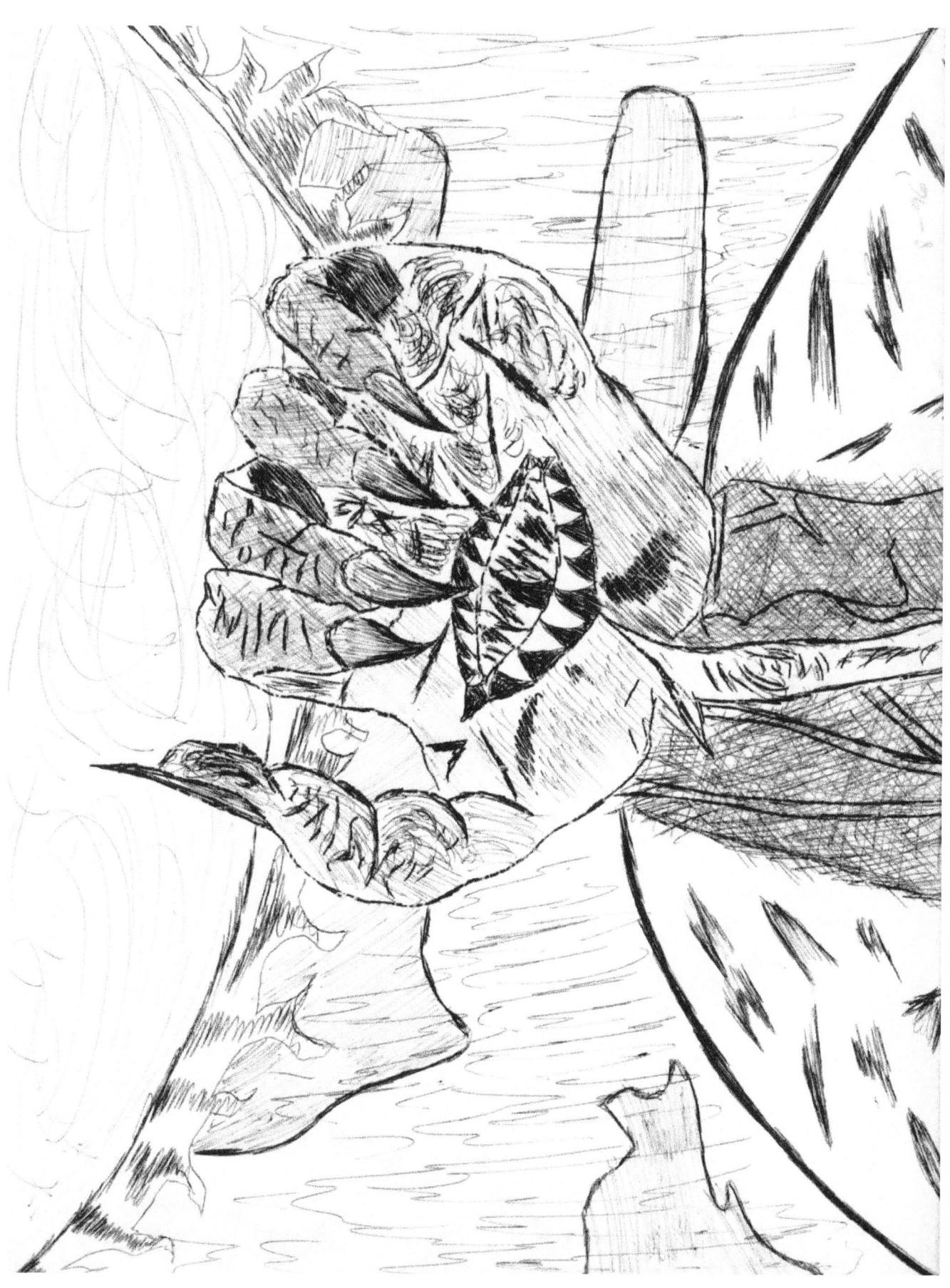

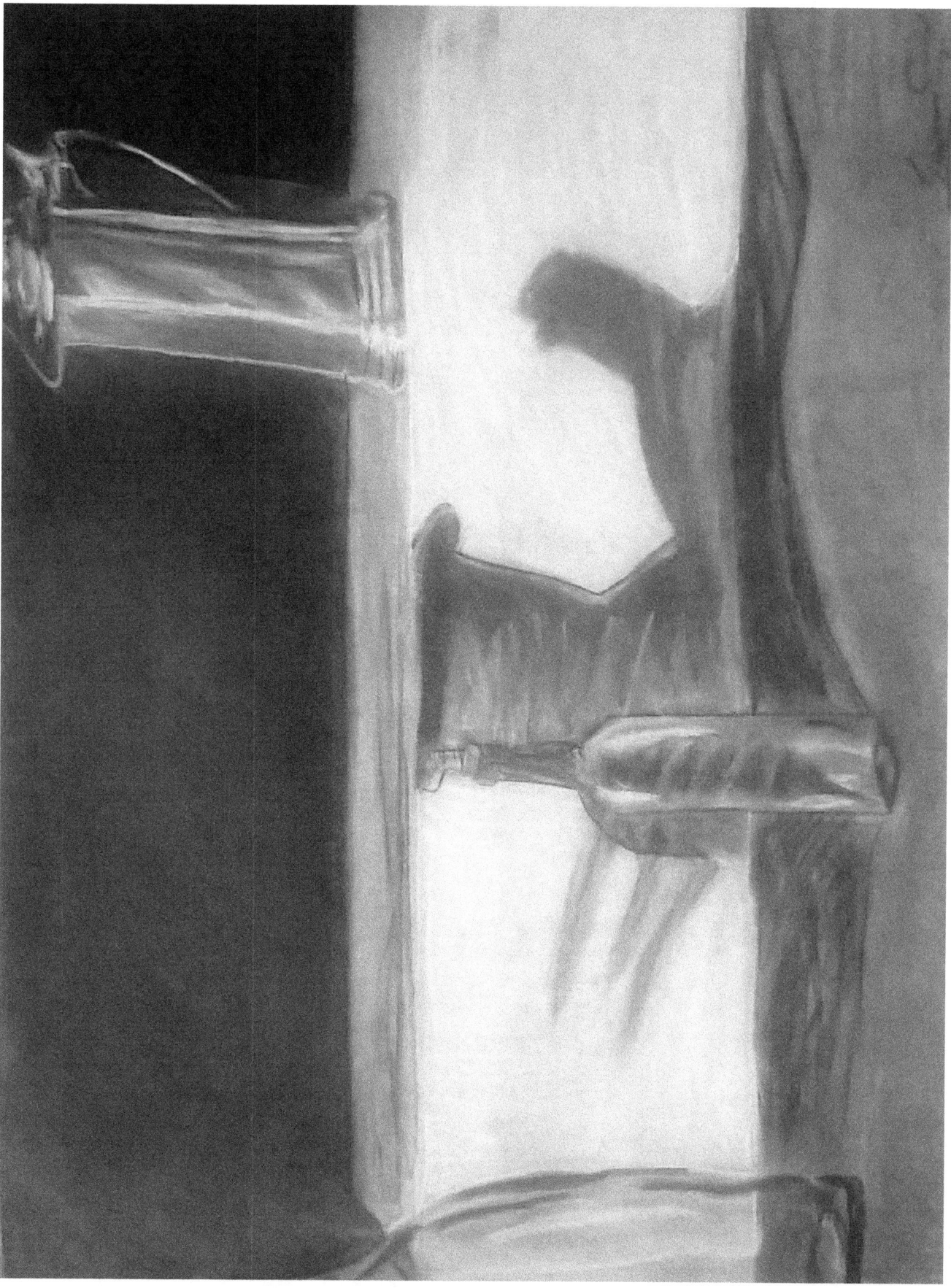

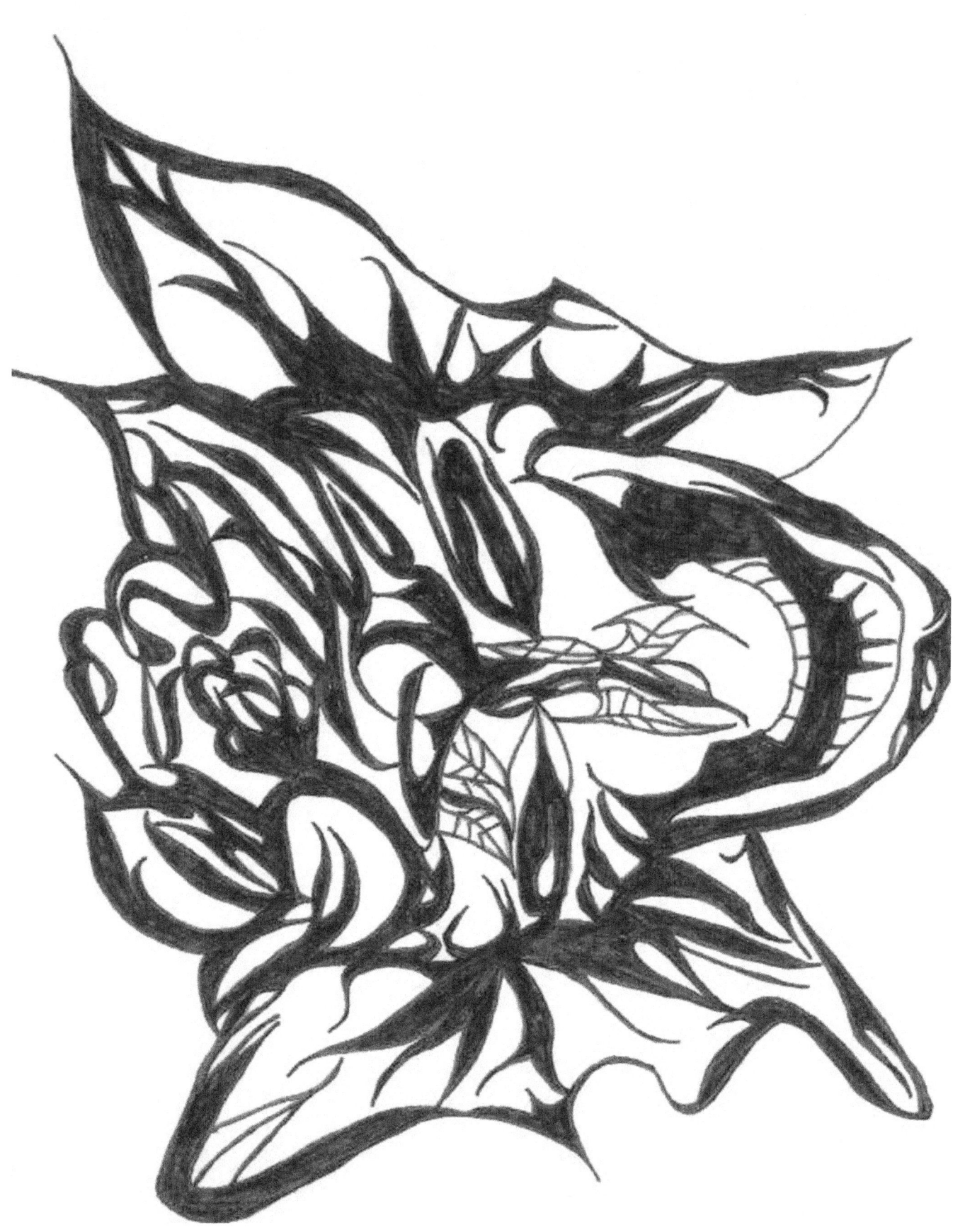

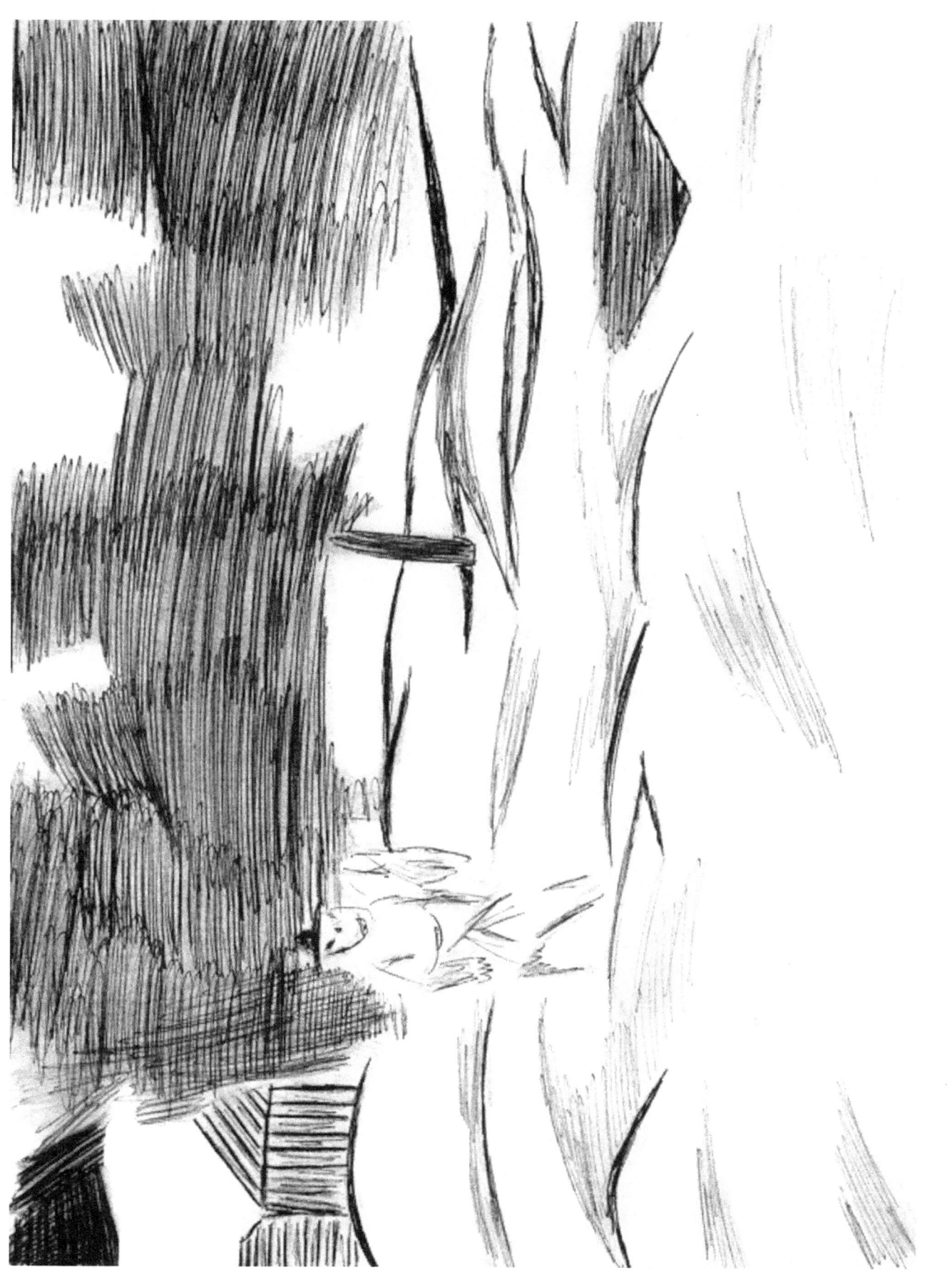

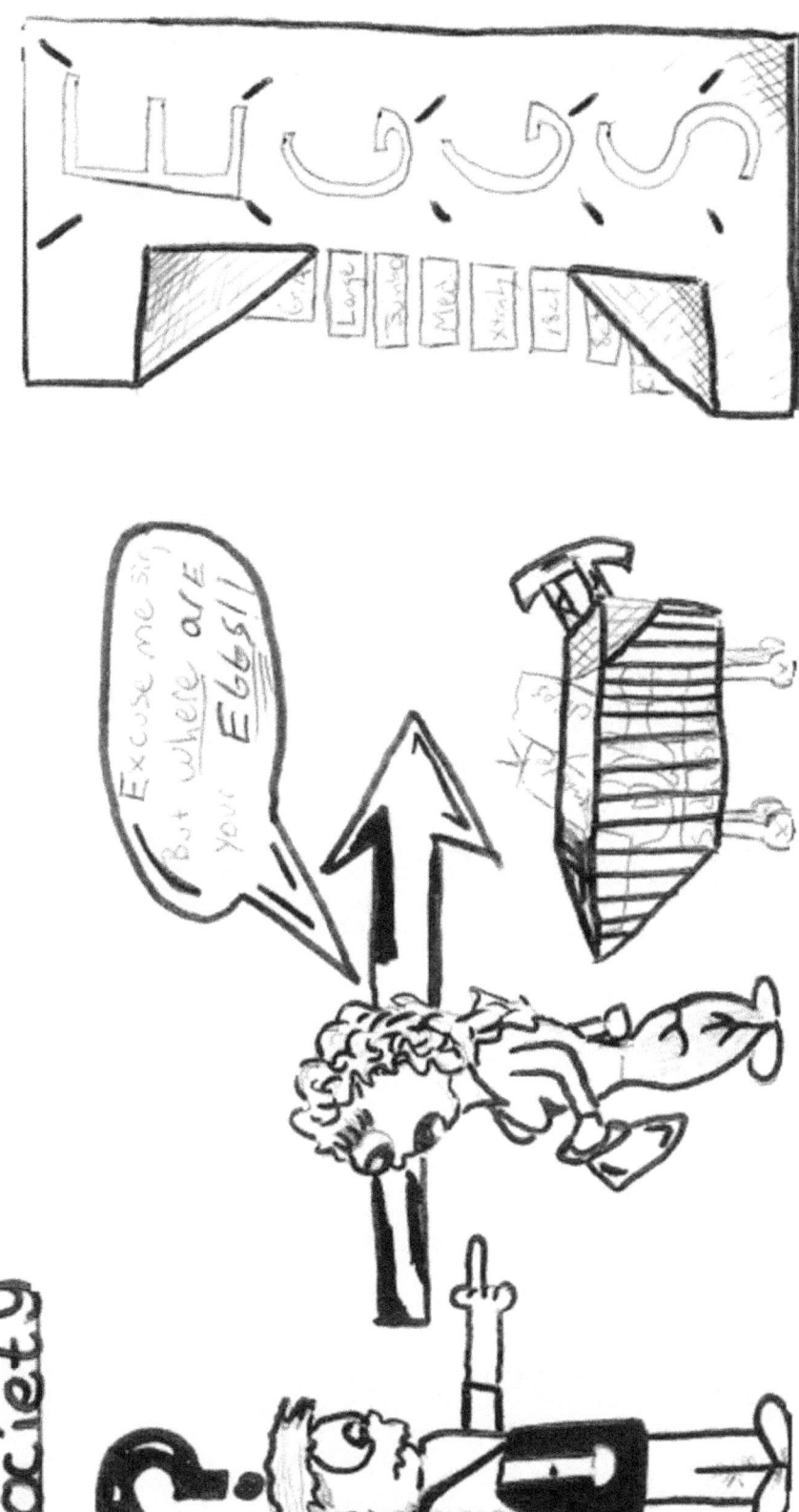

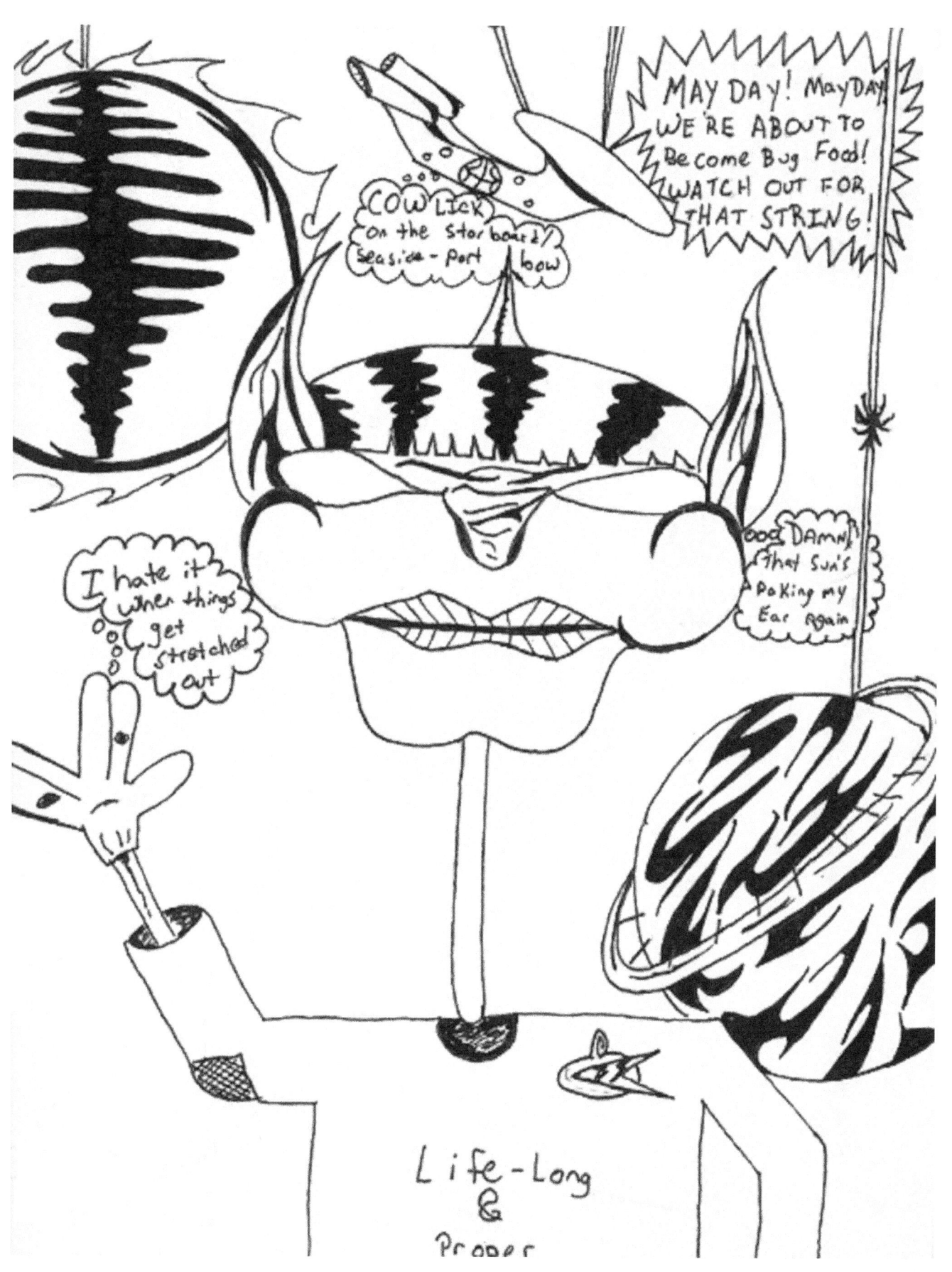

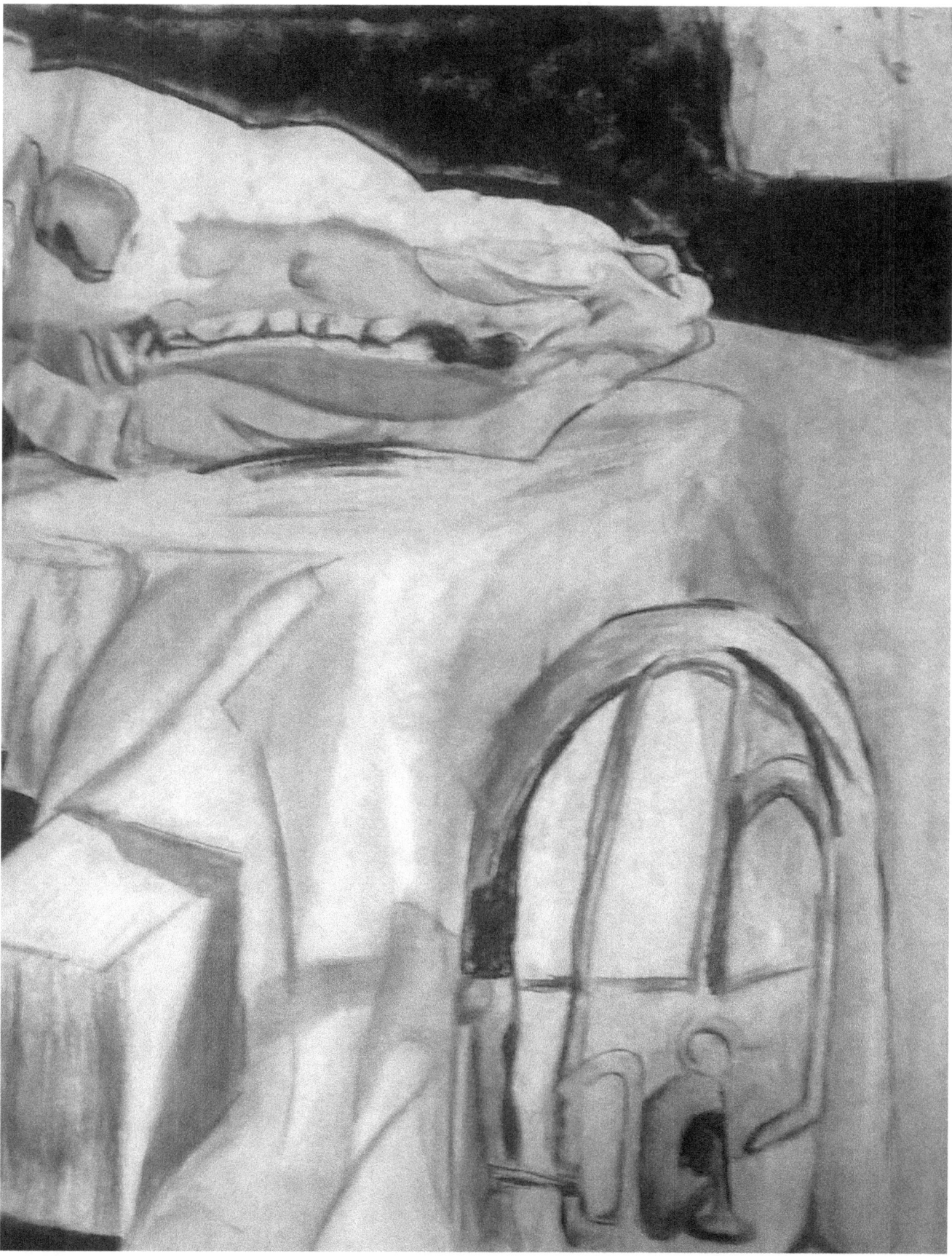

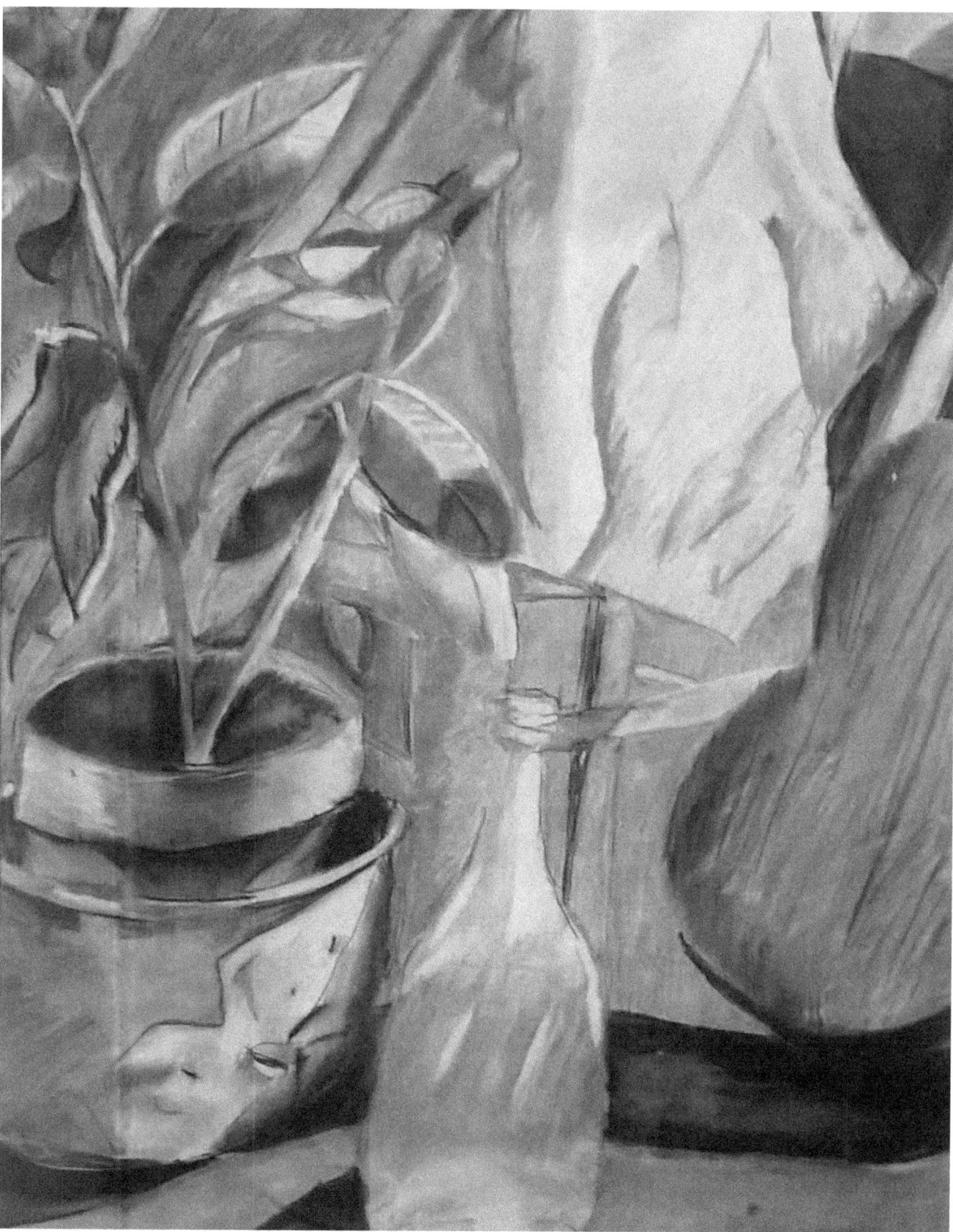

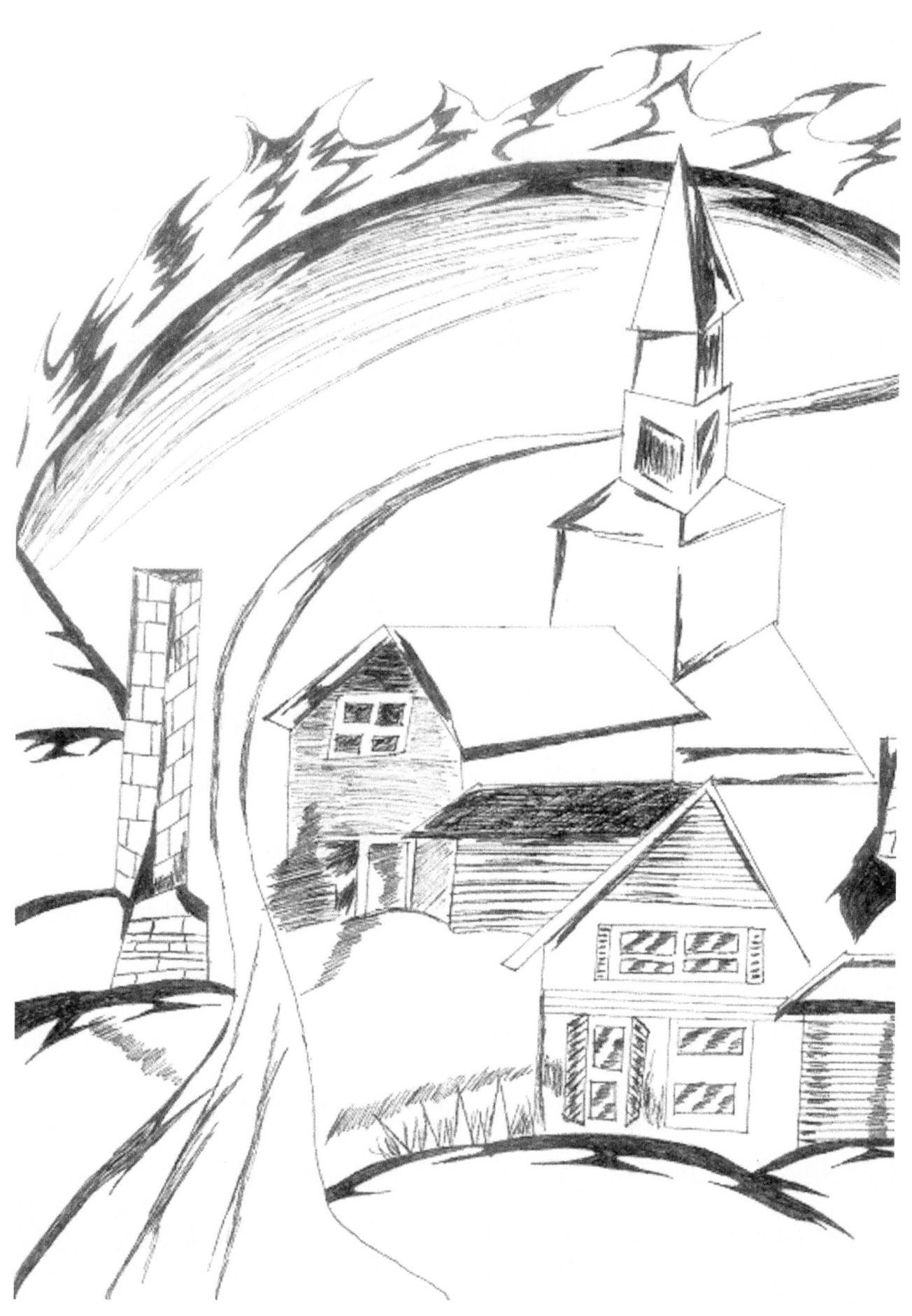

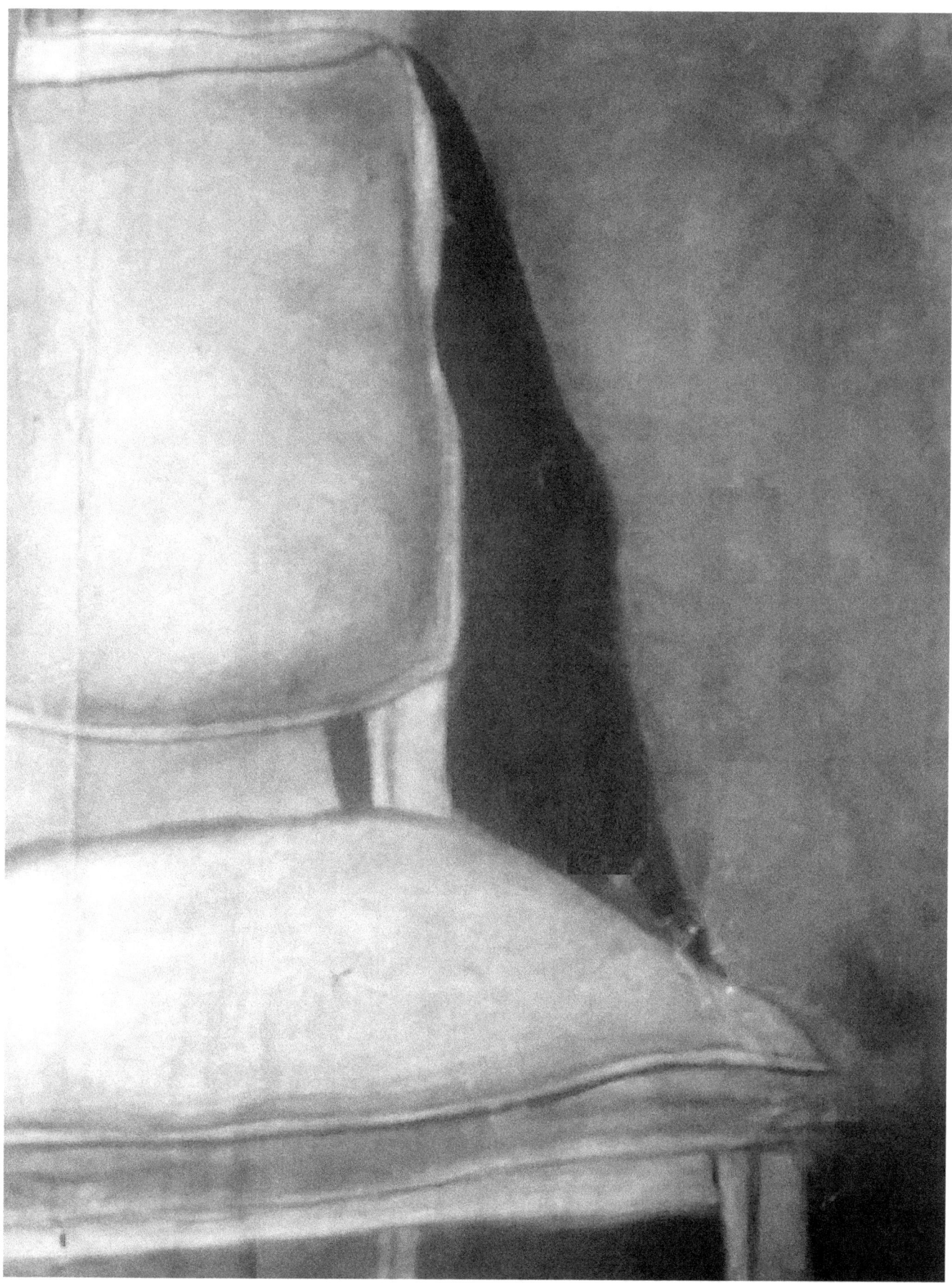

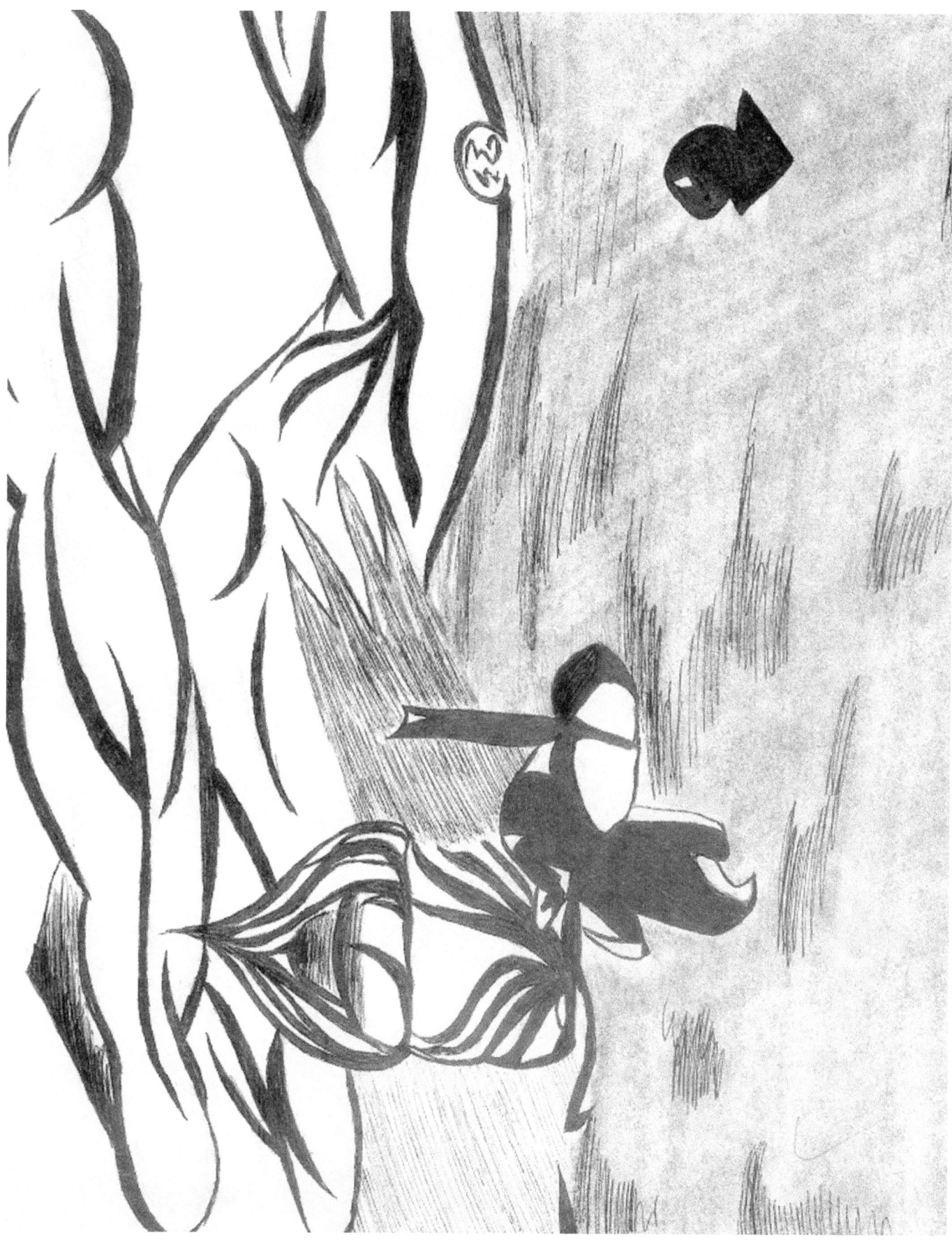

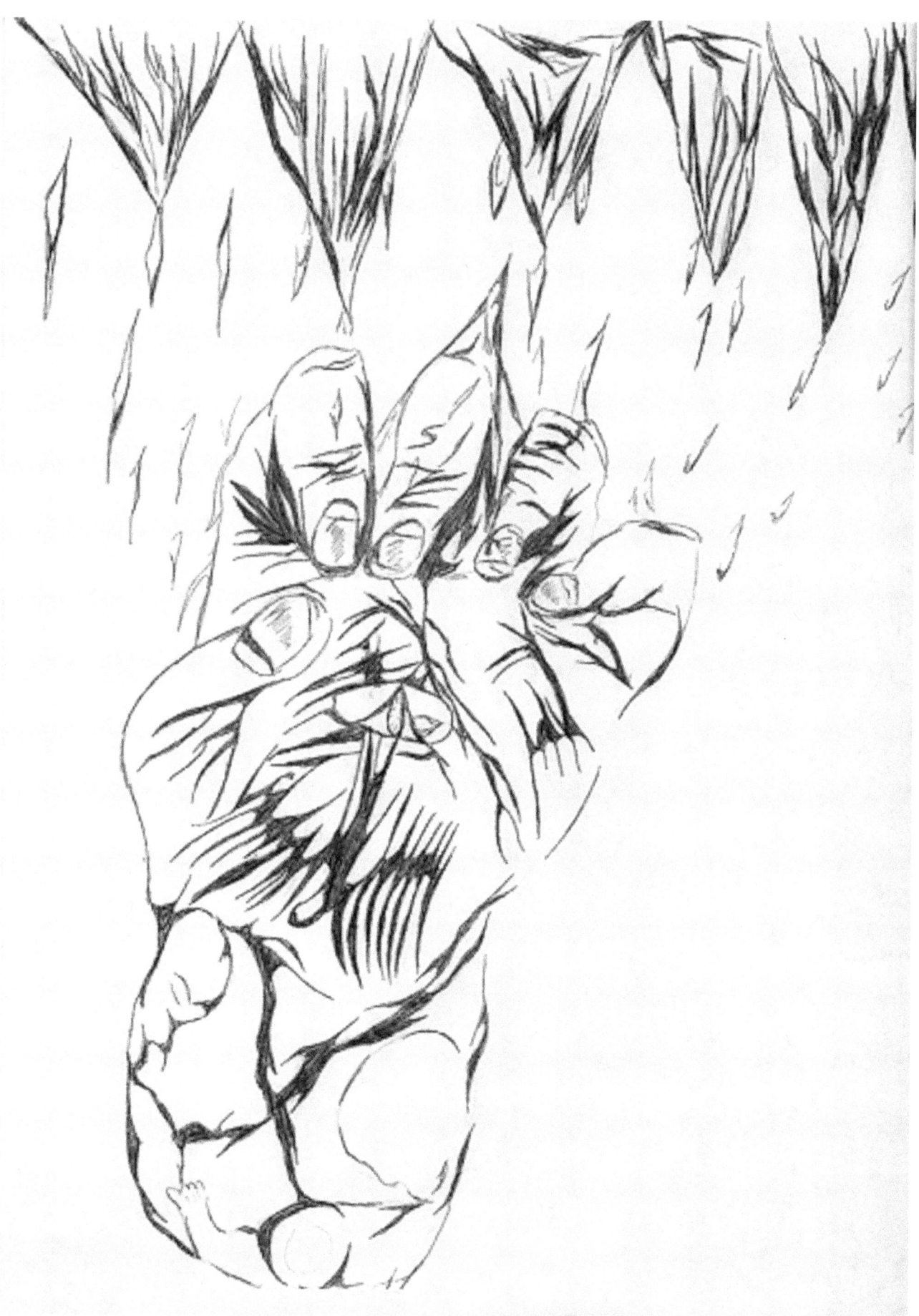

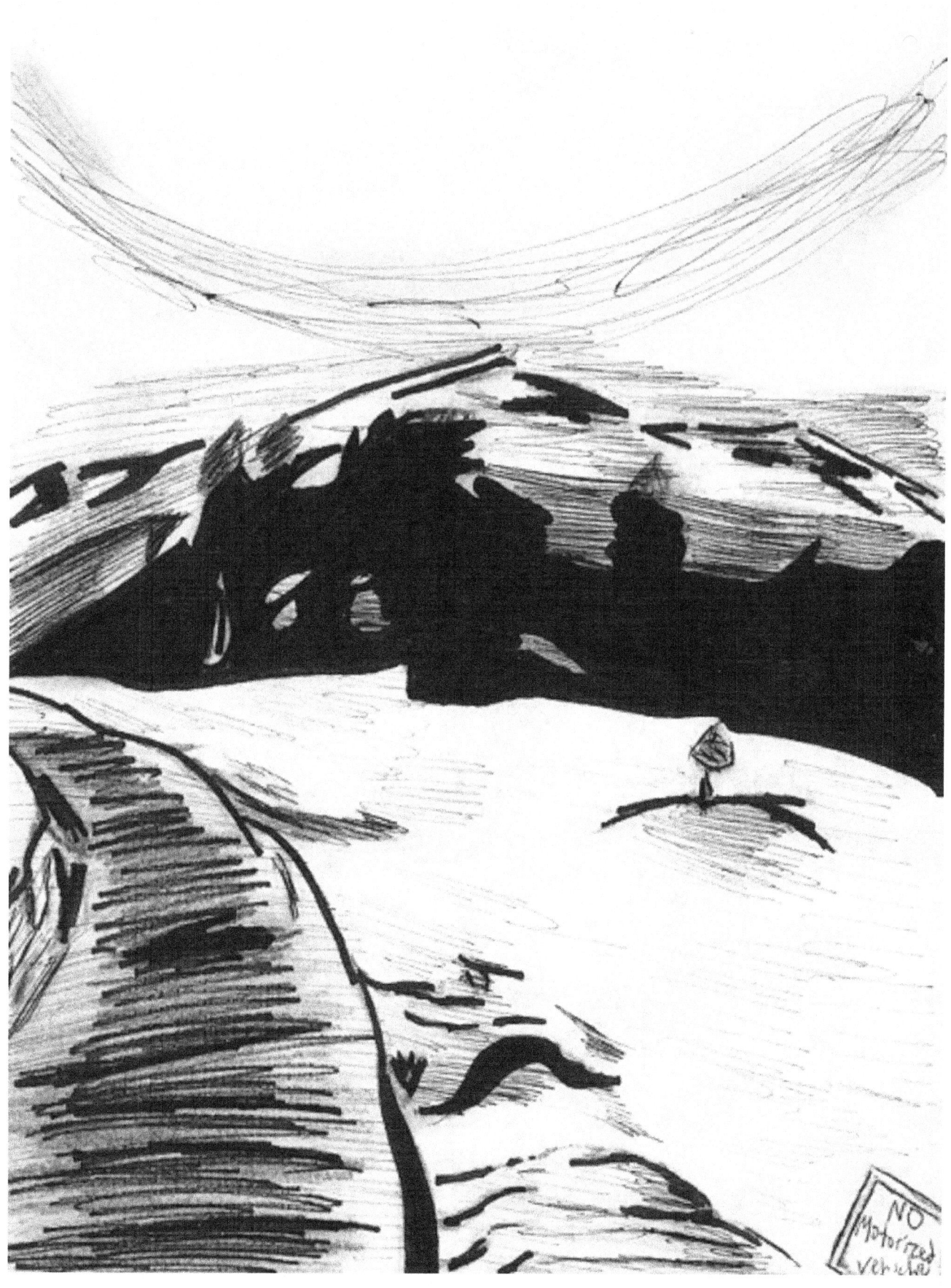

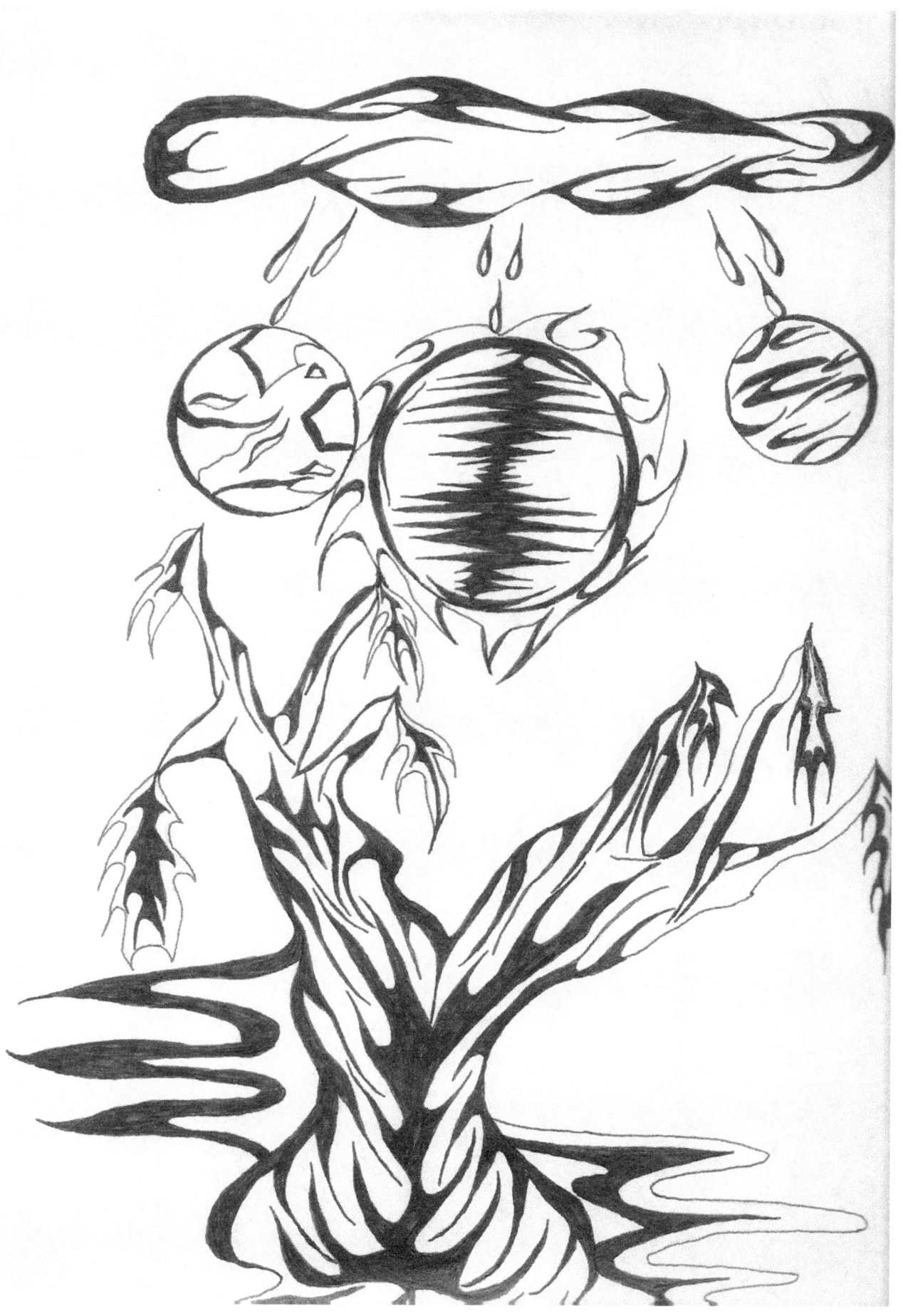

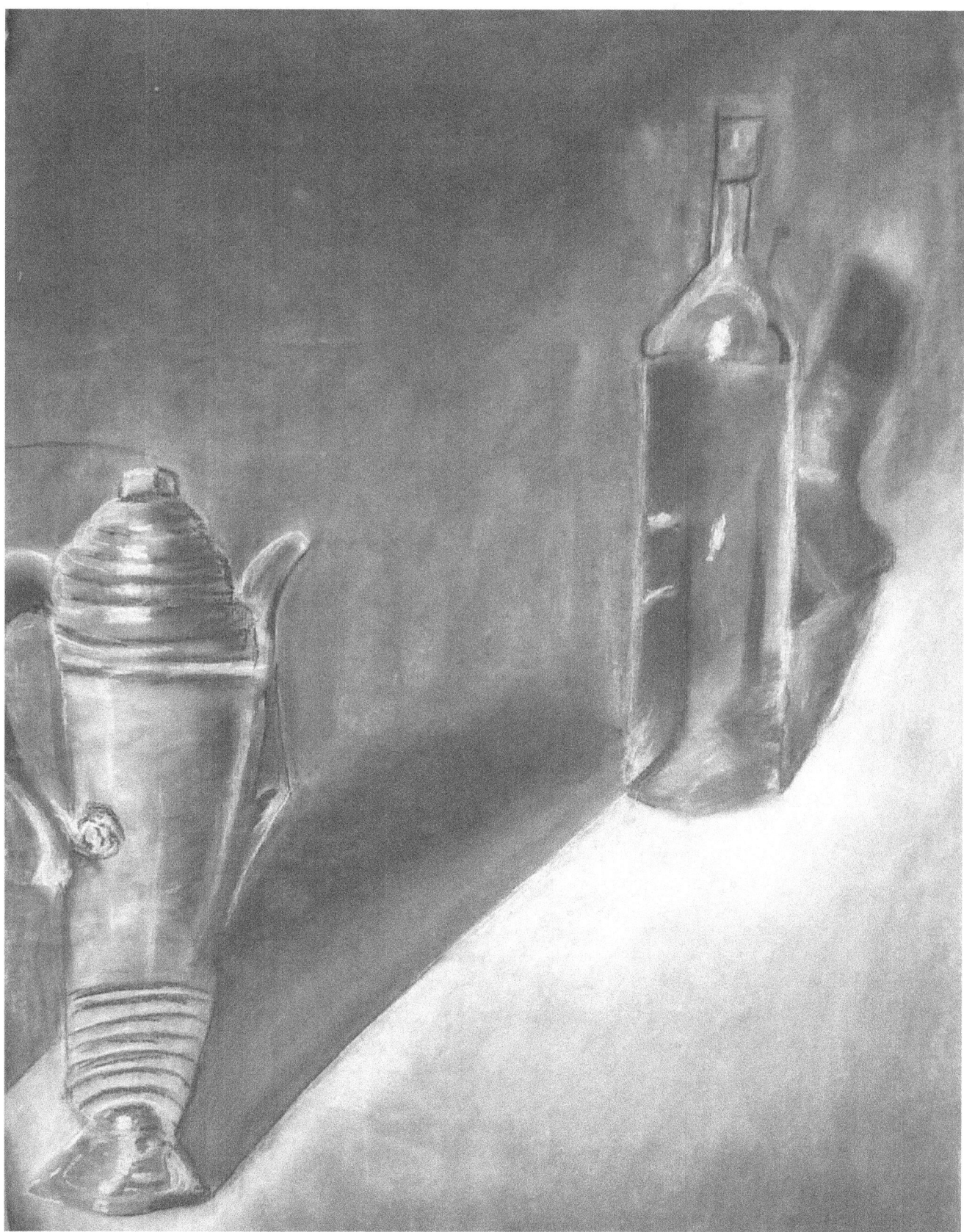

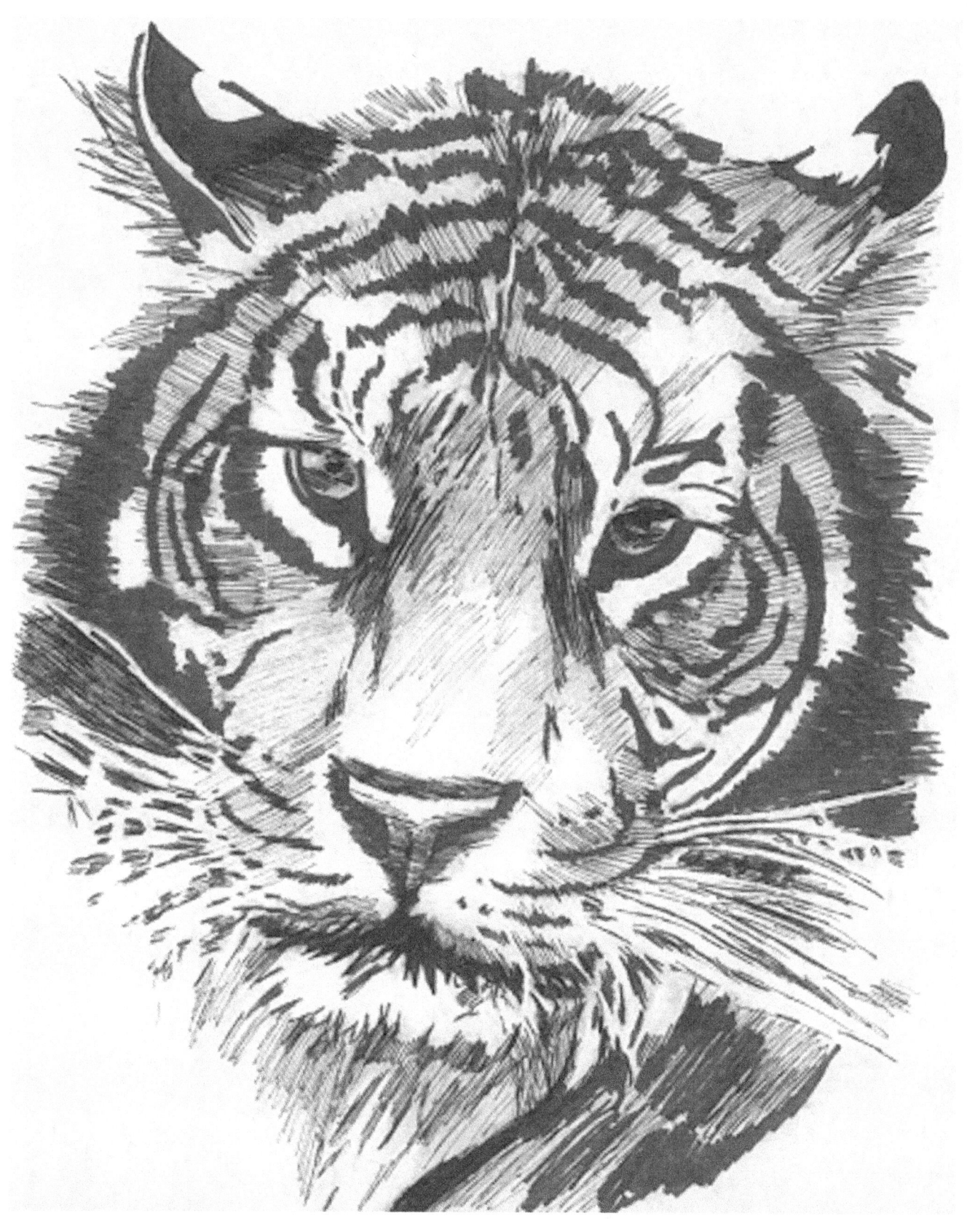

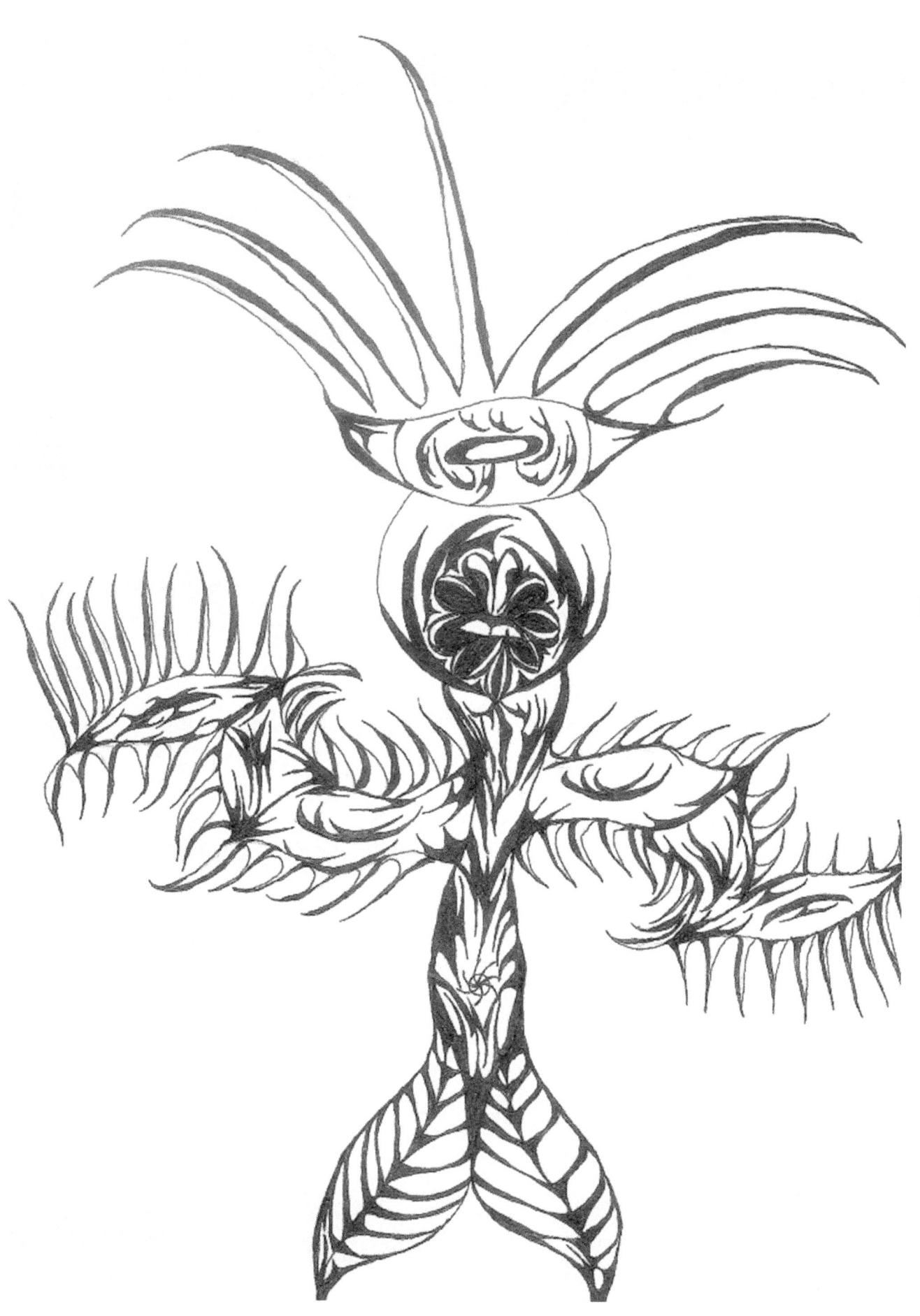

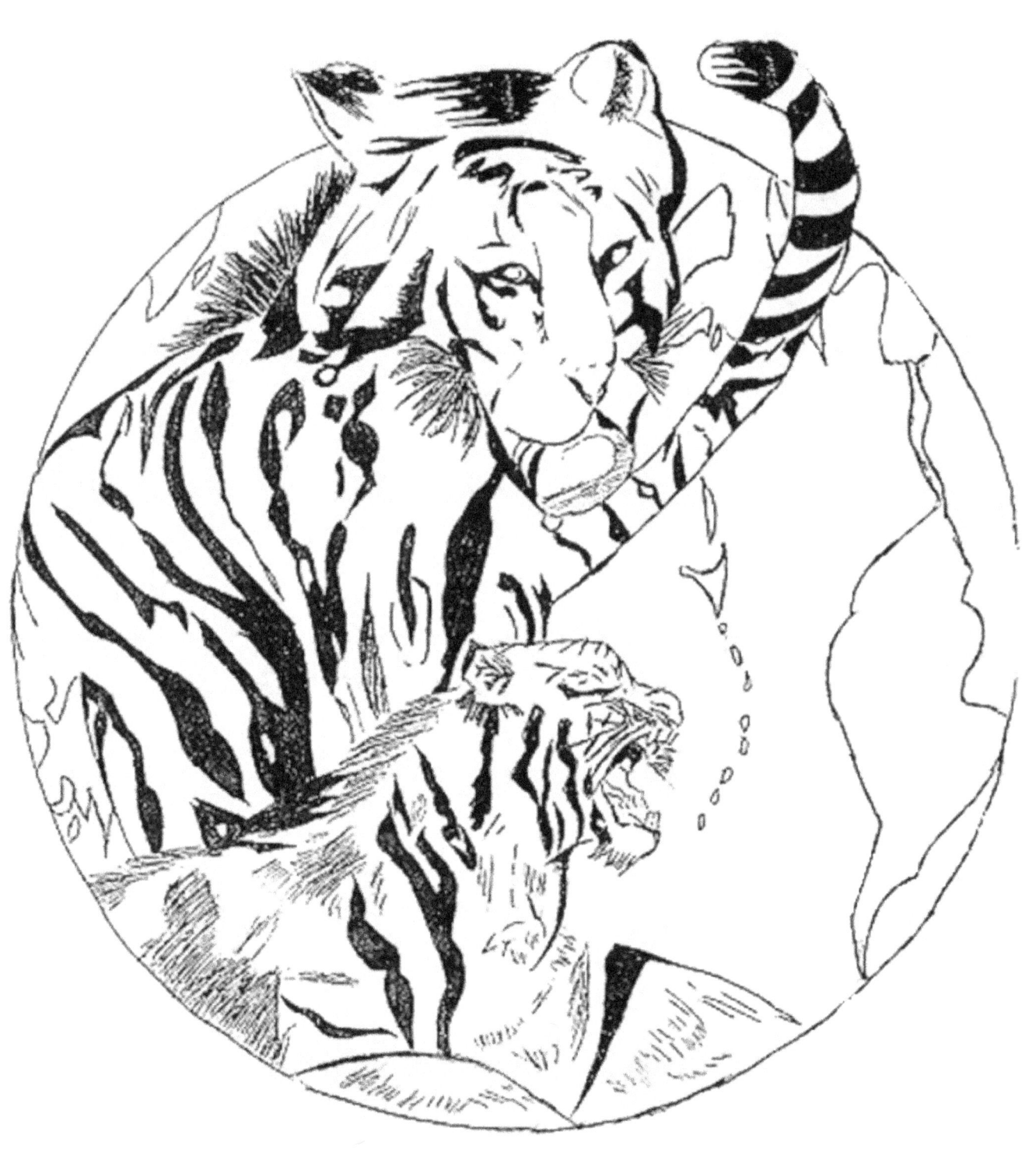

Apprentice Edition Bonus Selections

The following selections are traced versions of earlier versions of work shown in the standard portion of this collection. They may also be incomplete versions, or various stages leading to the final work. This section is included here to allow you the opportunity to finish the works, adding your own spin to the work. Enjoy!!!

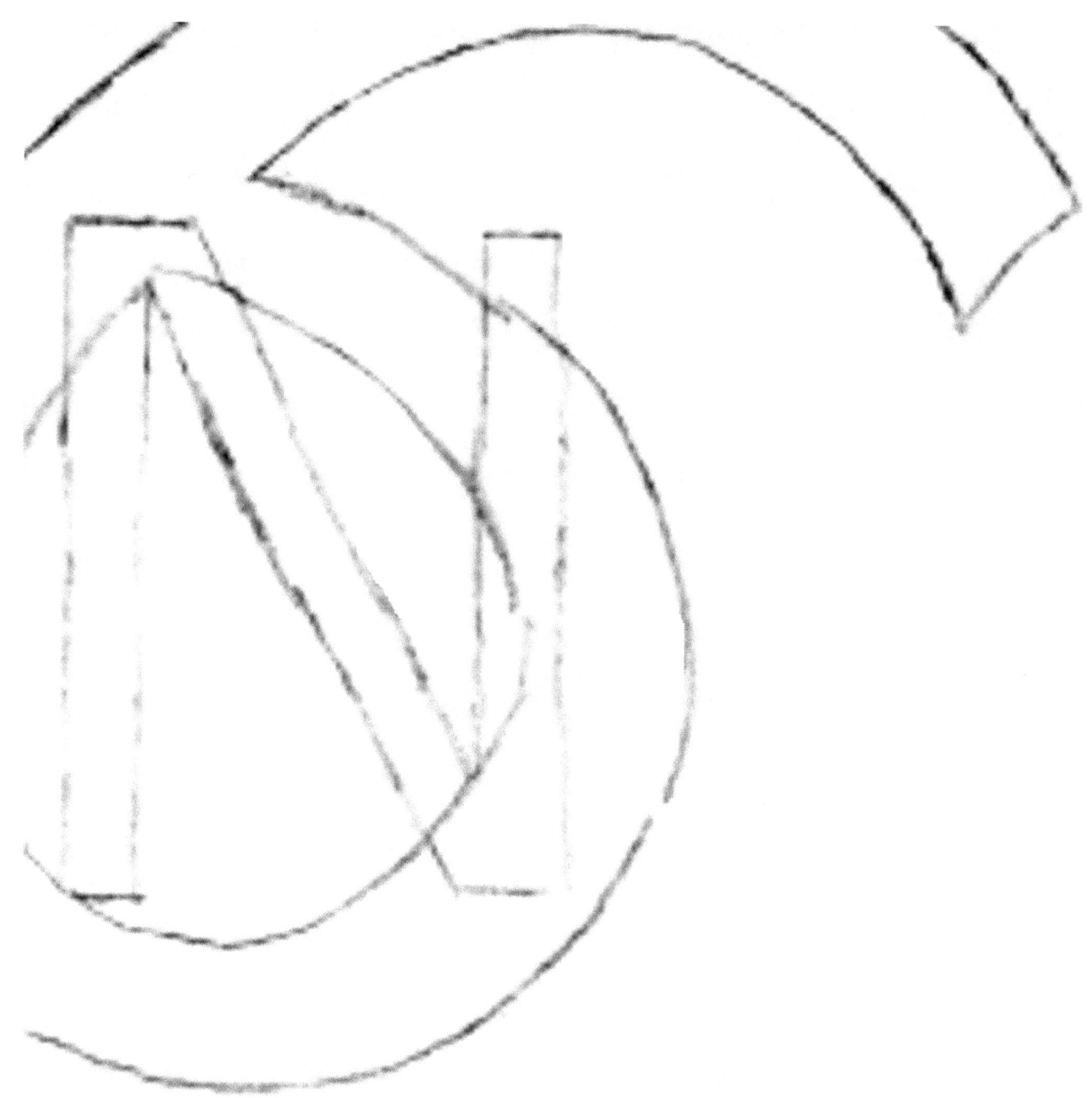

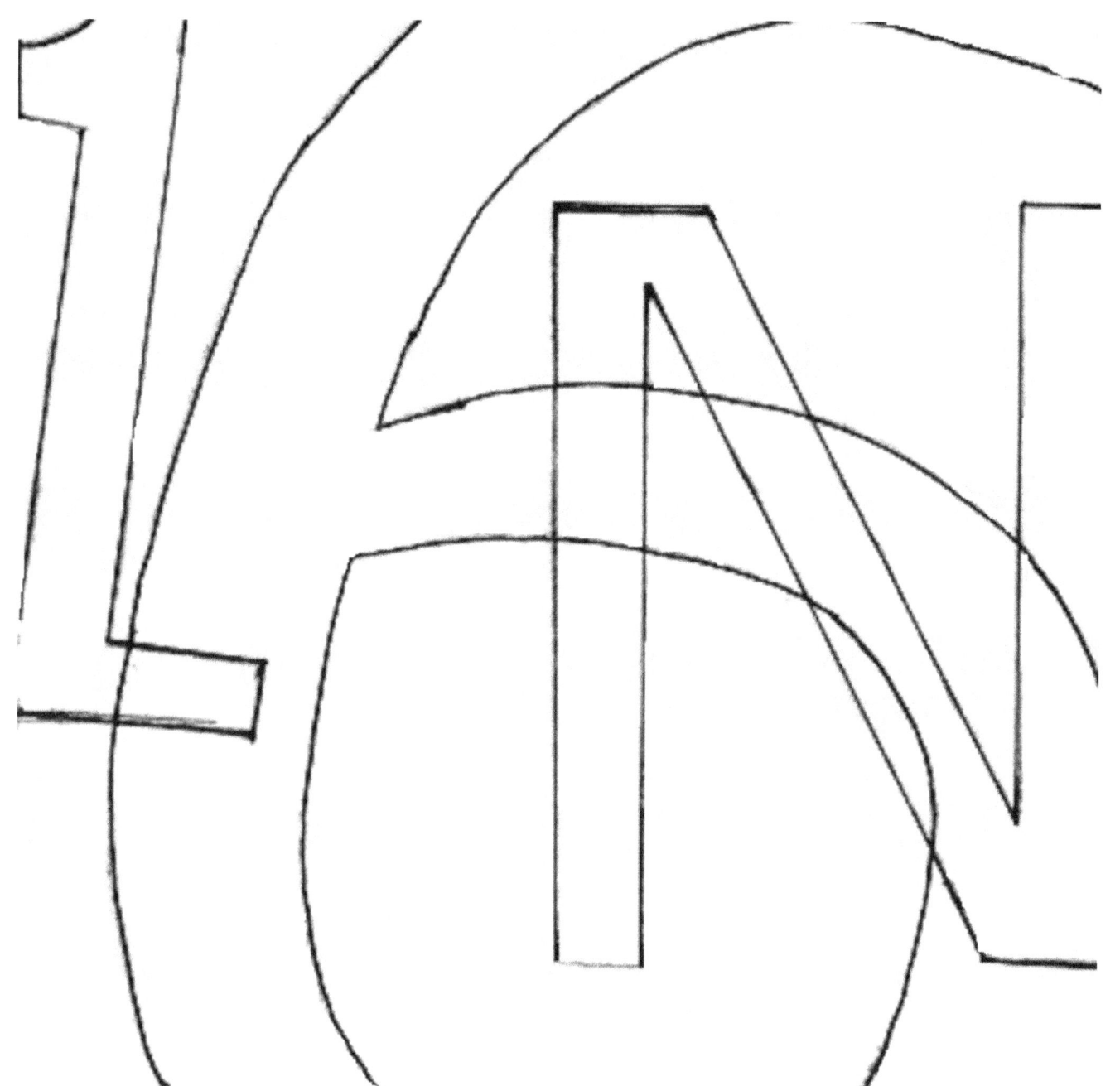

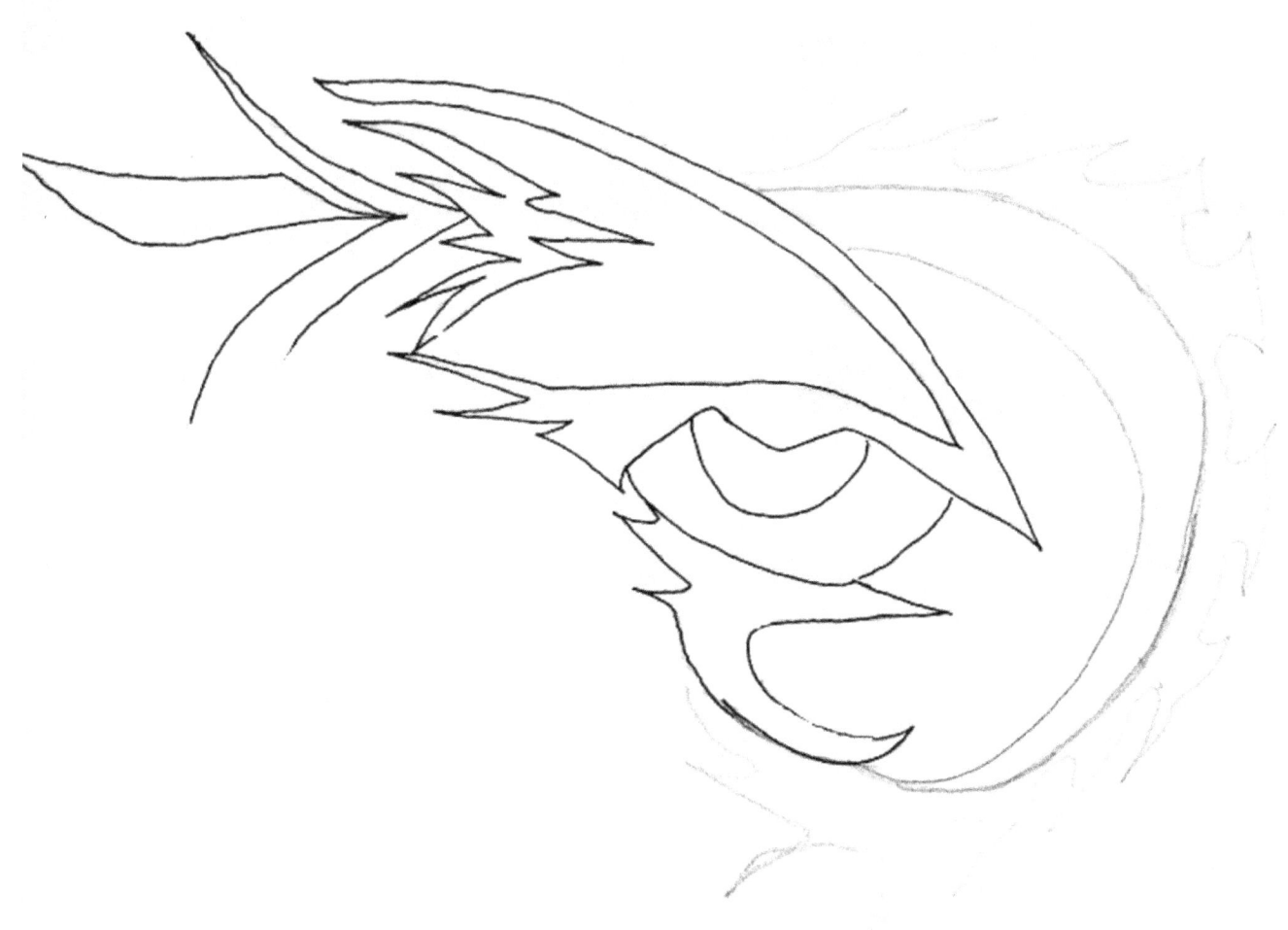

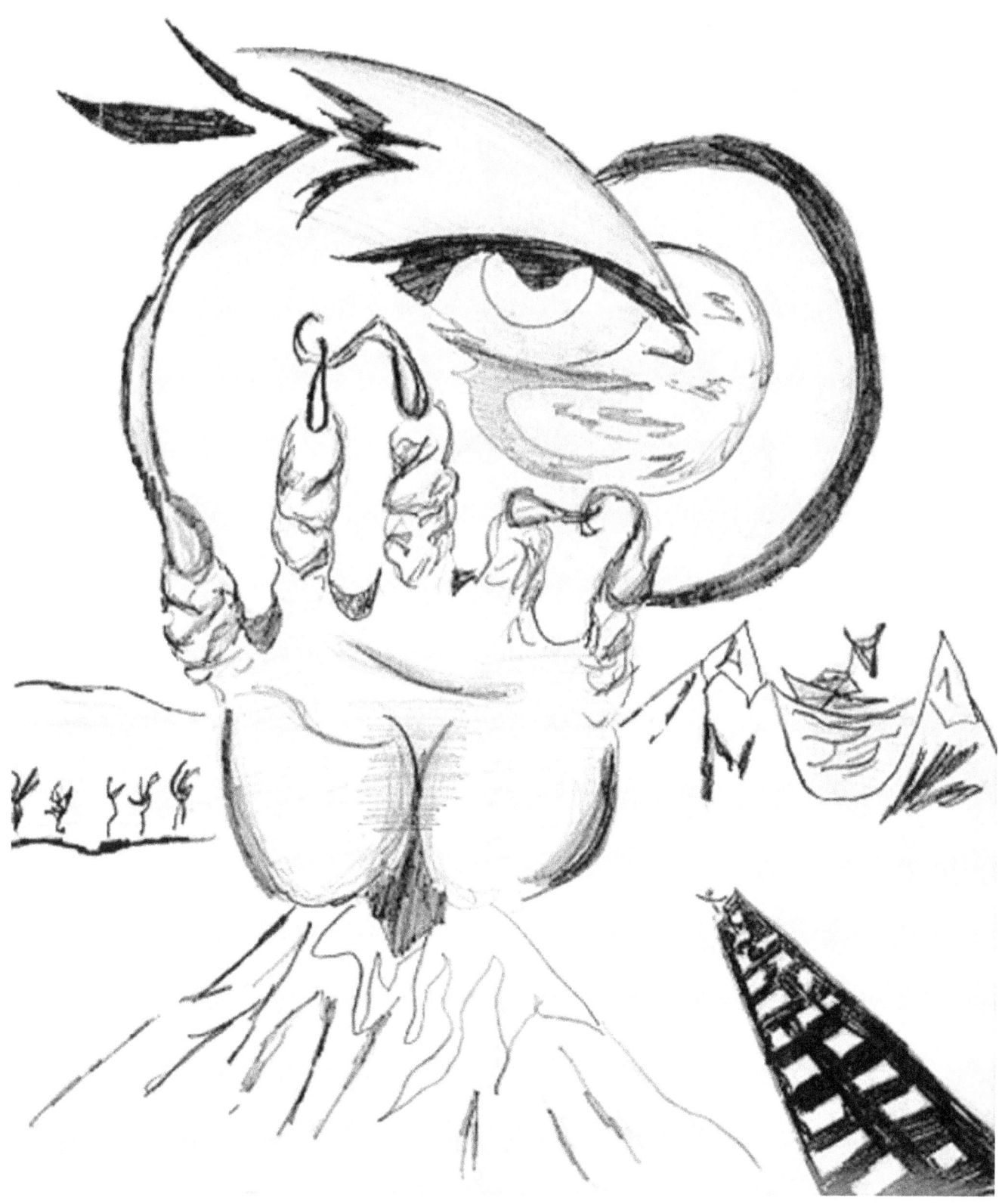

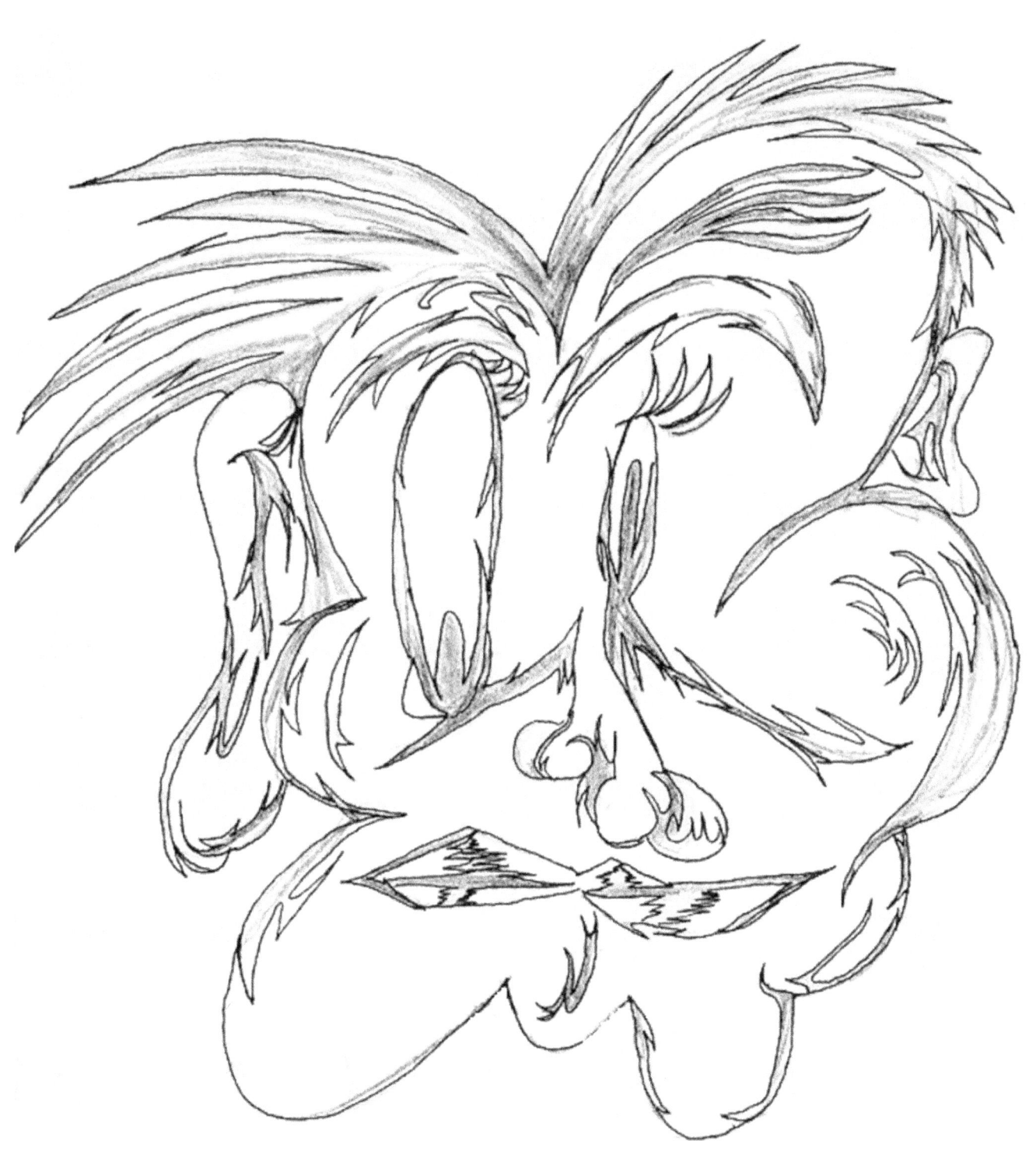

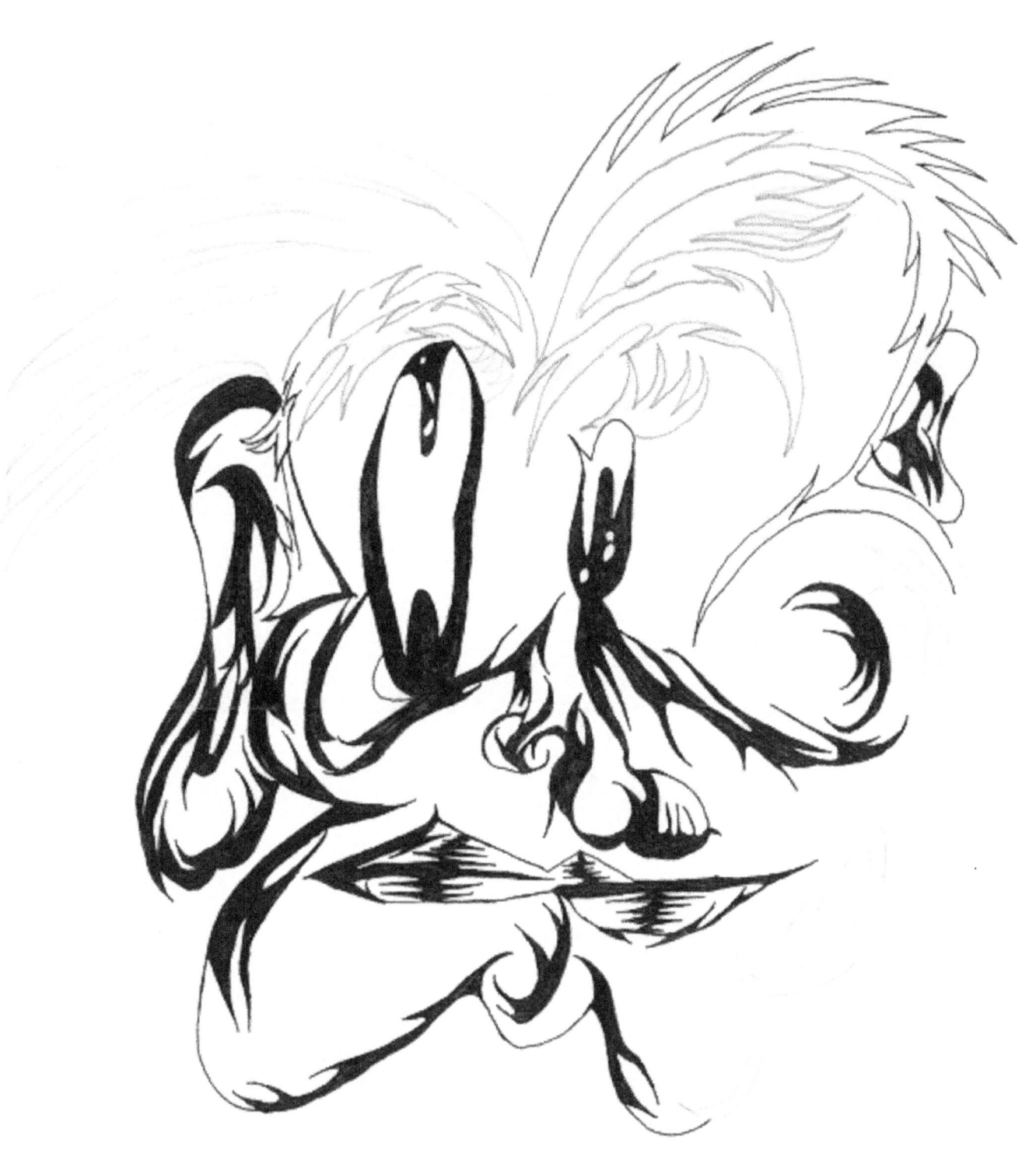

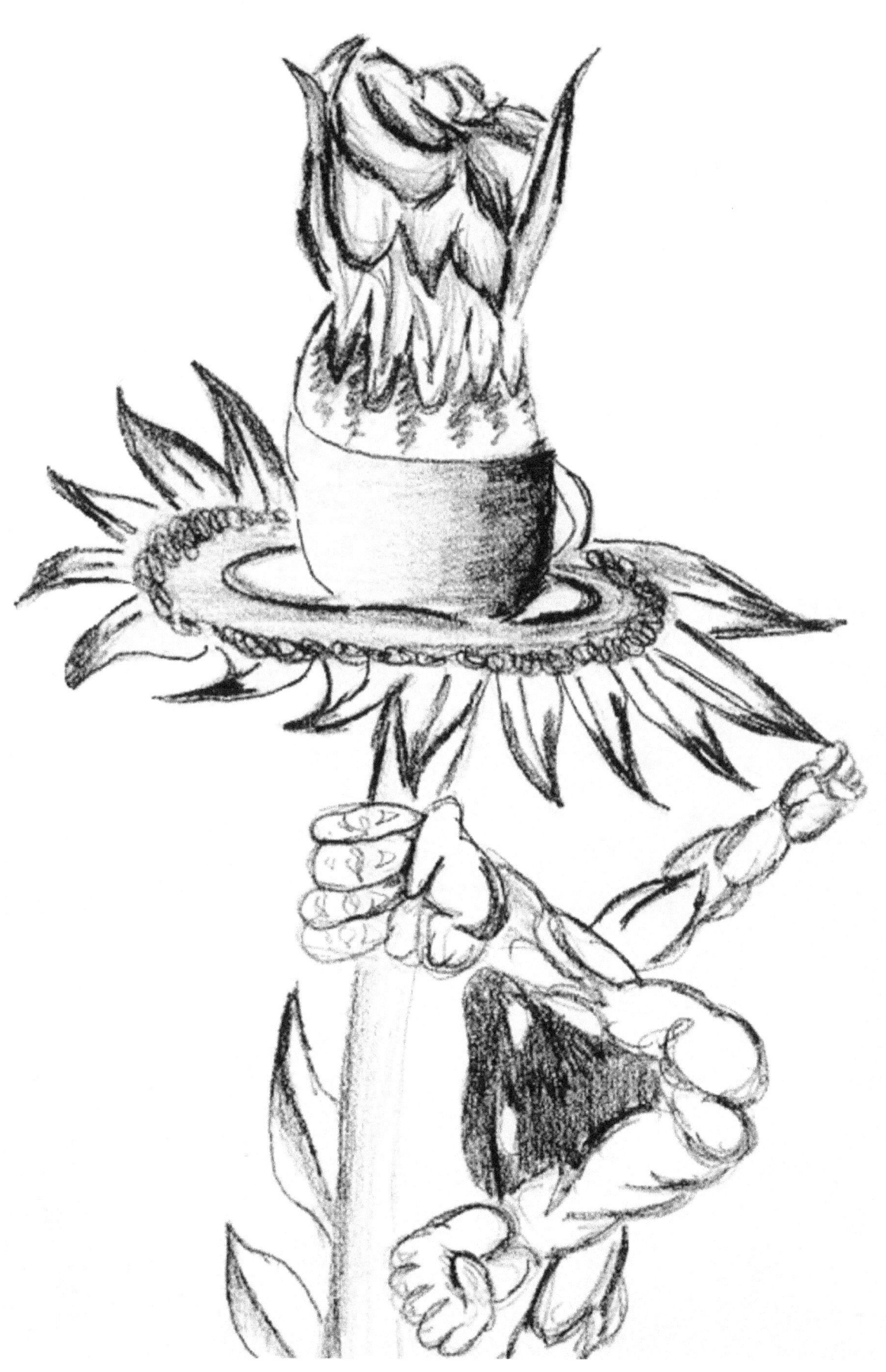

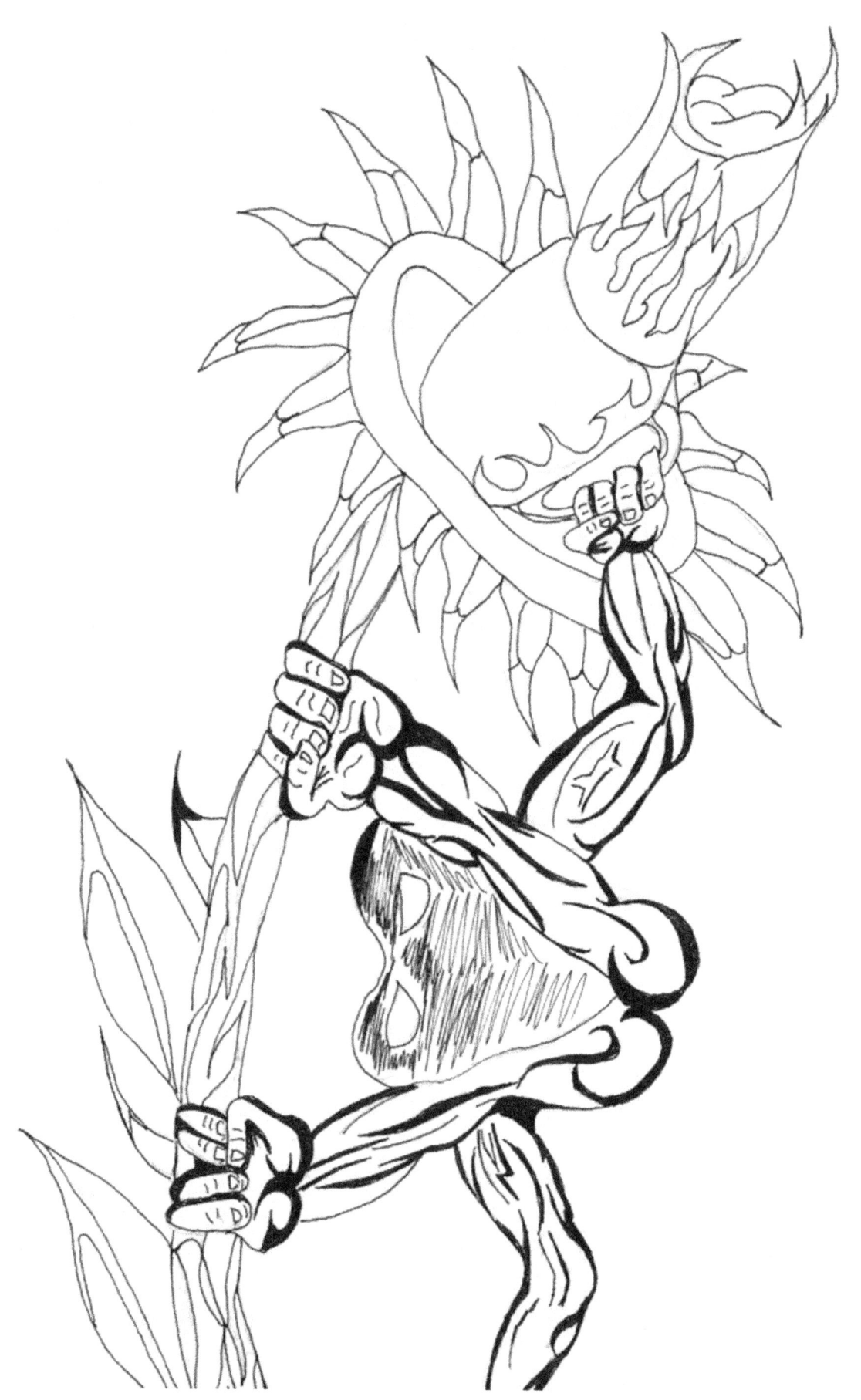

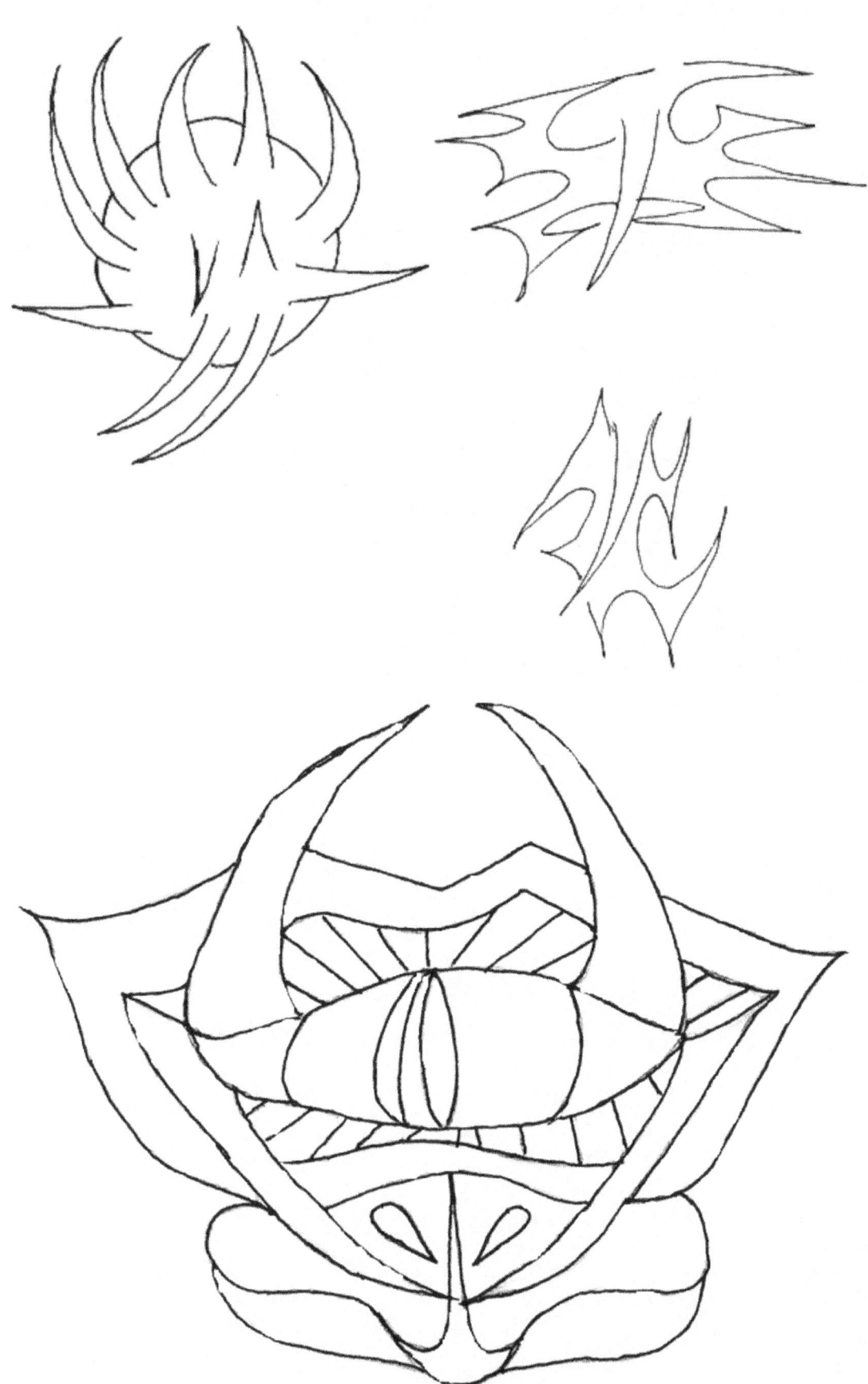

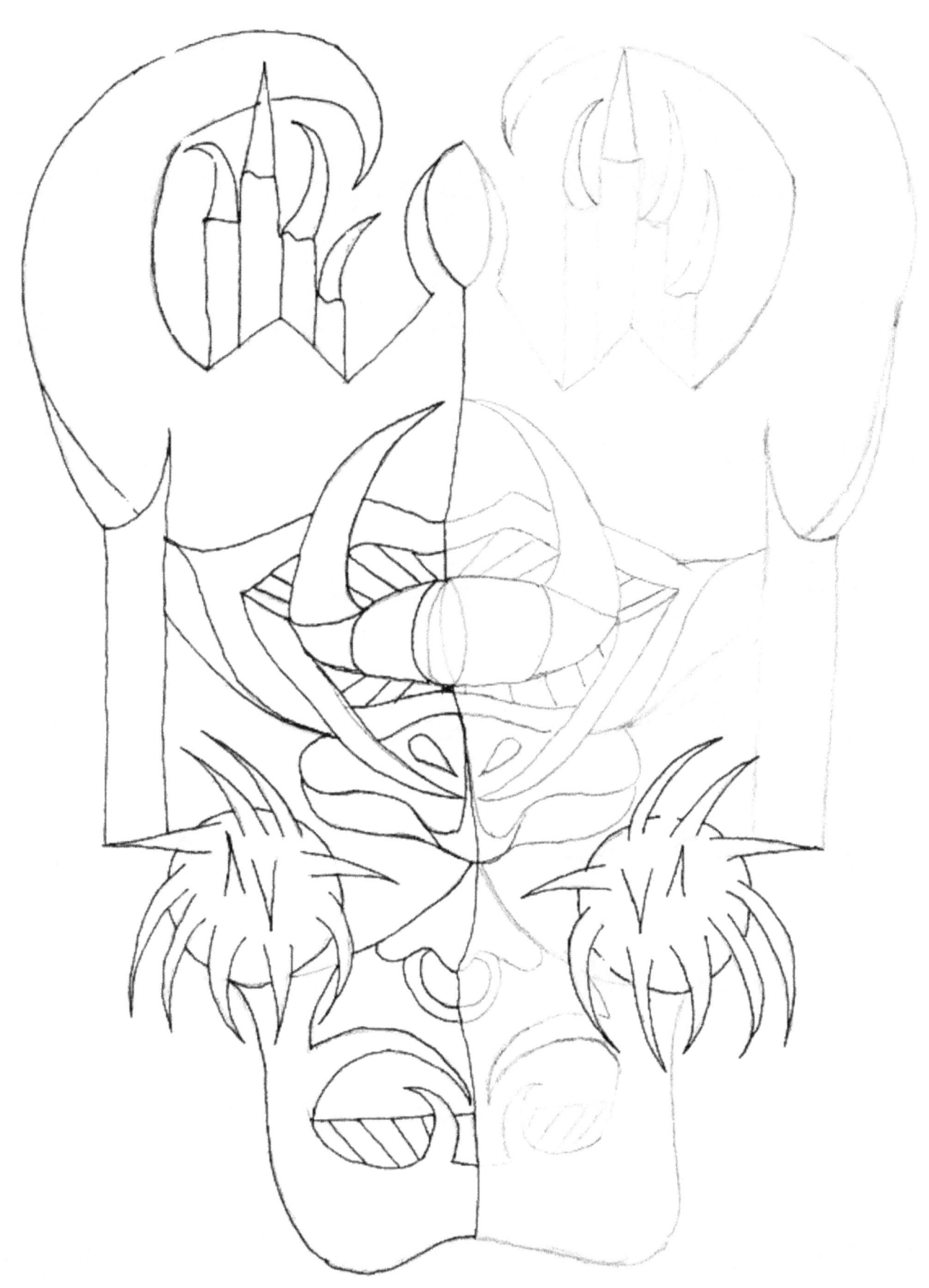

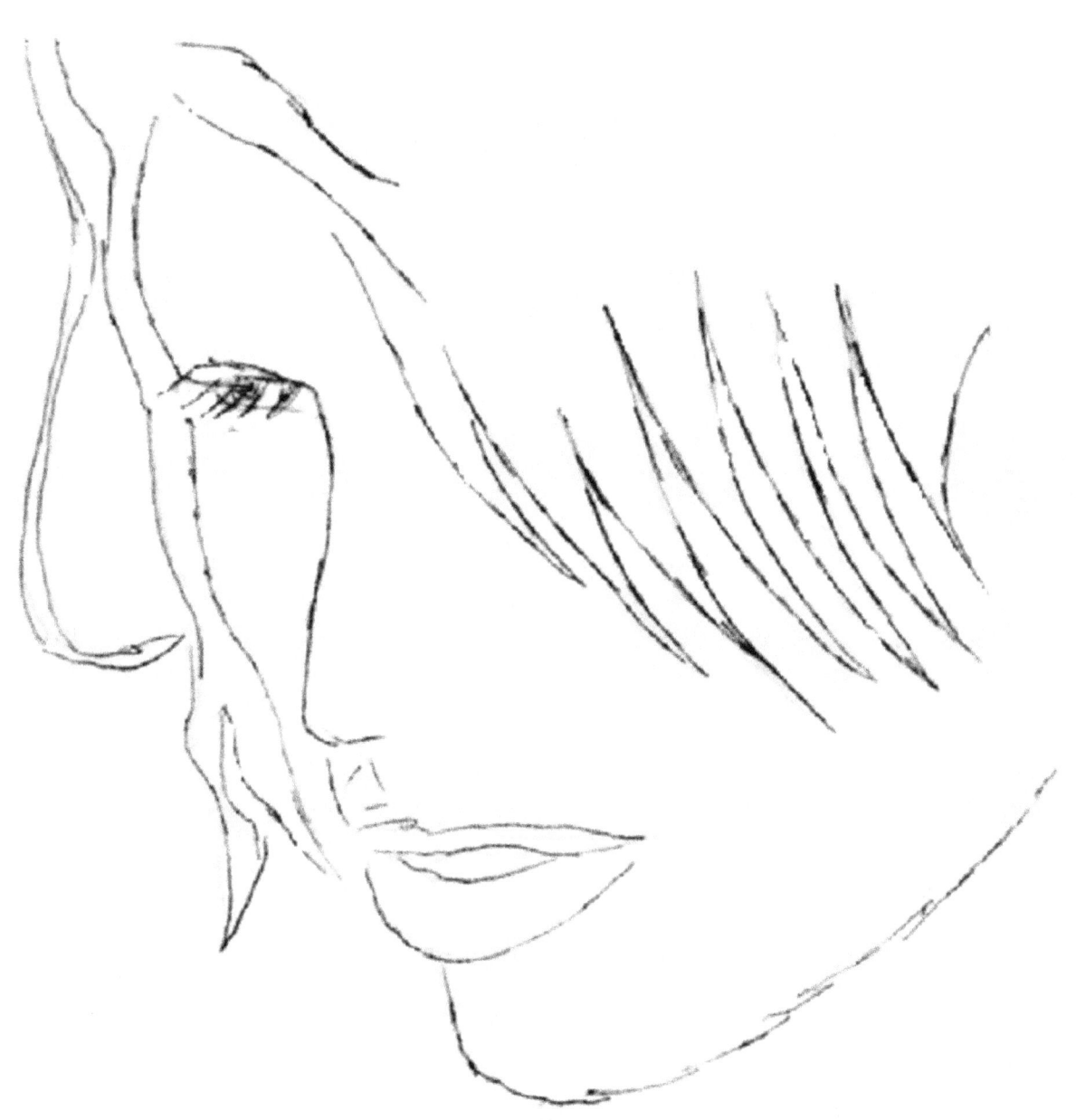

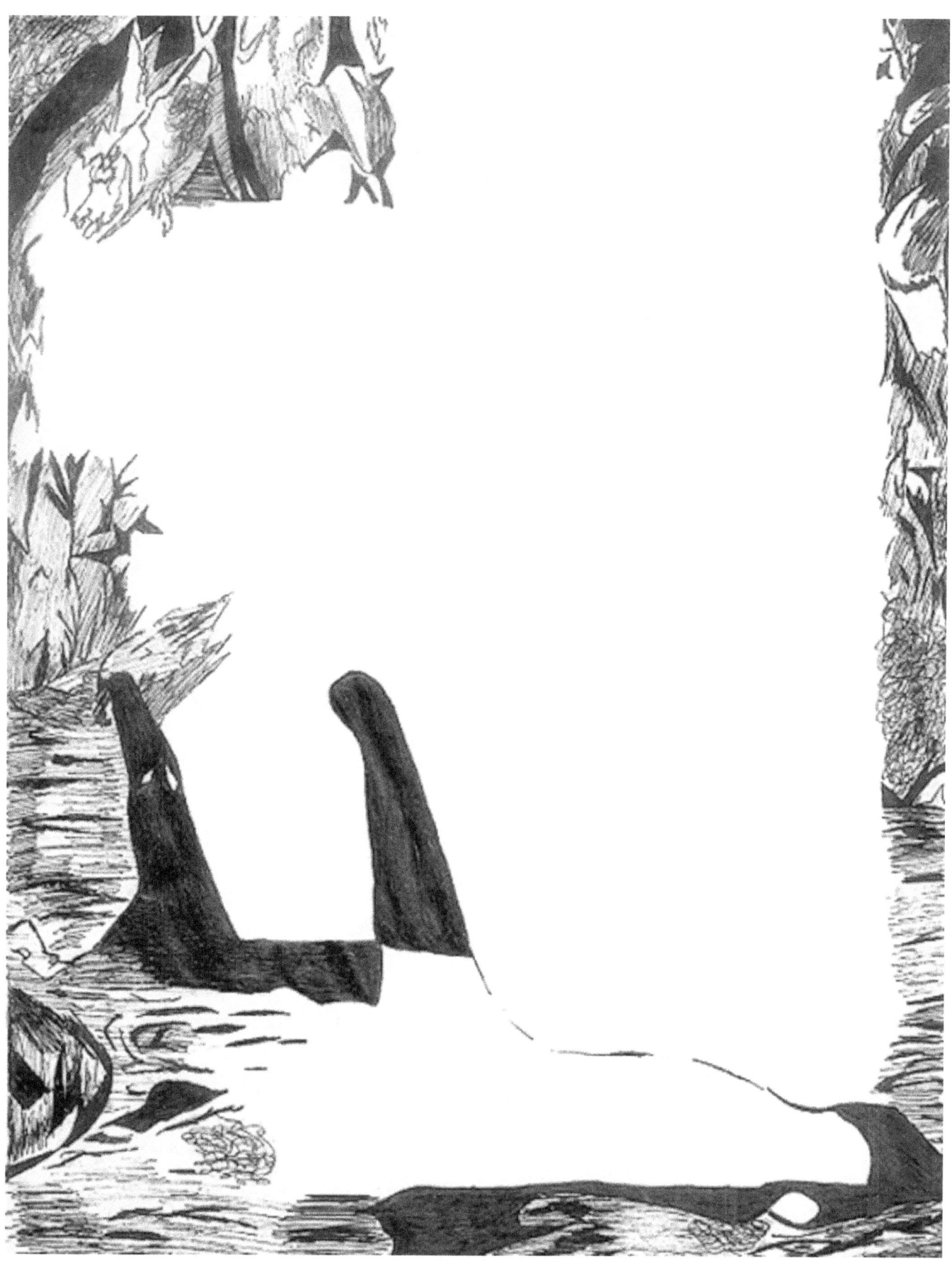

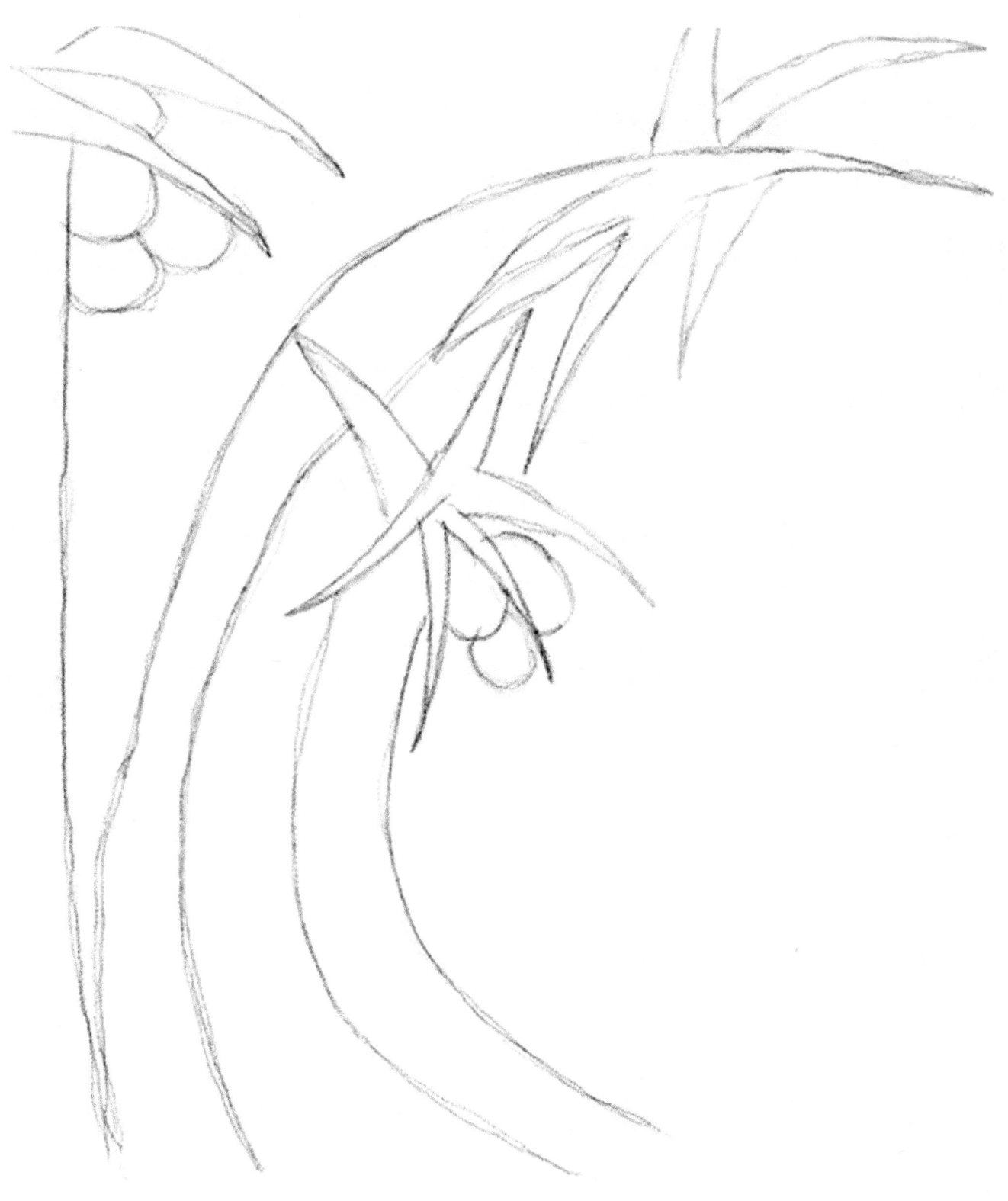

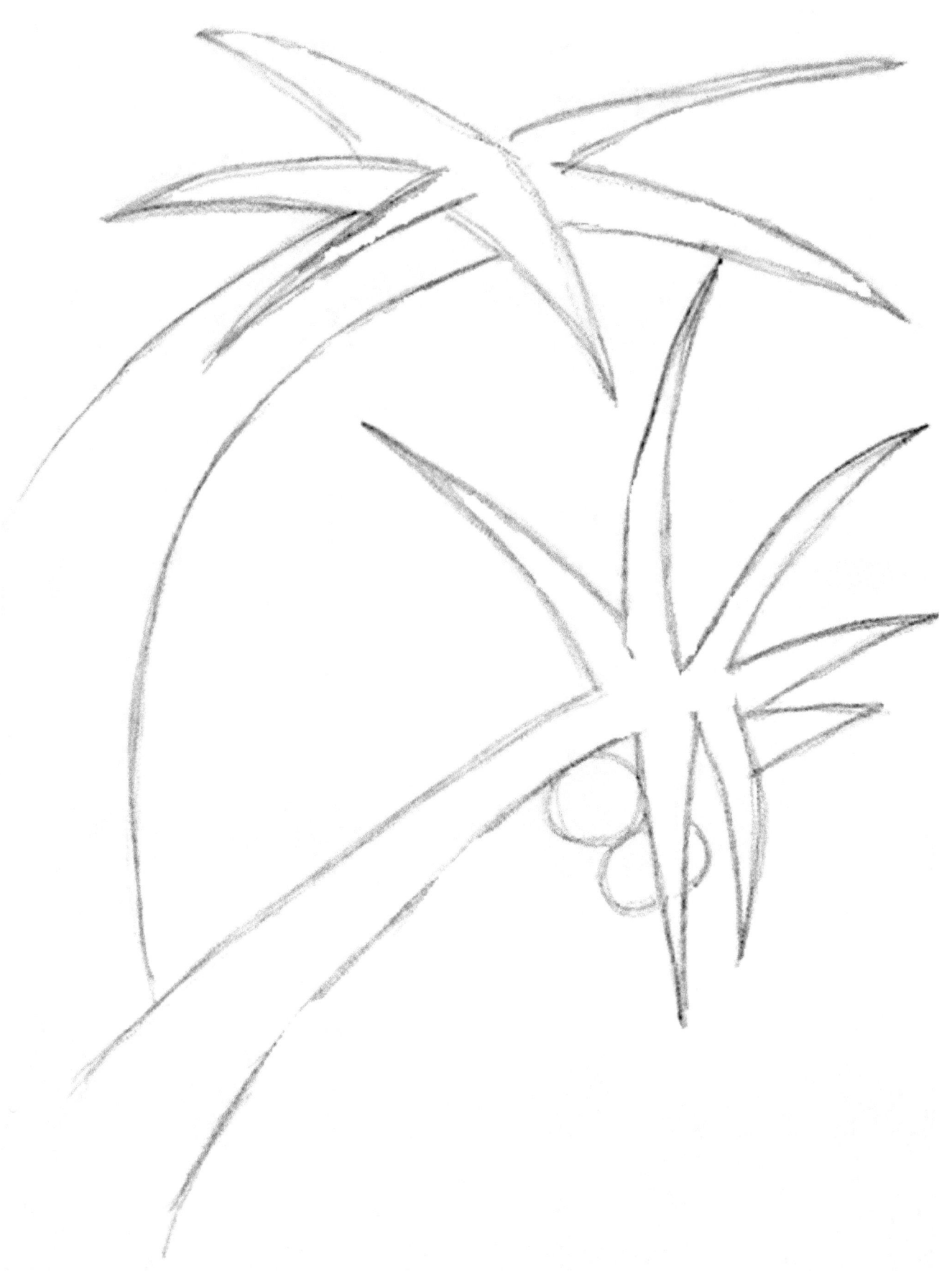

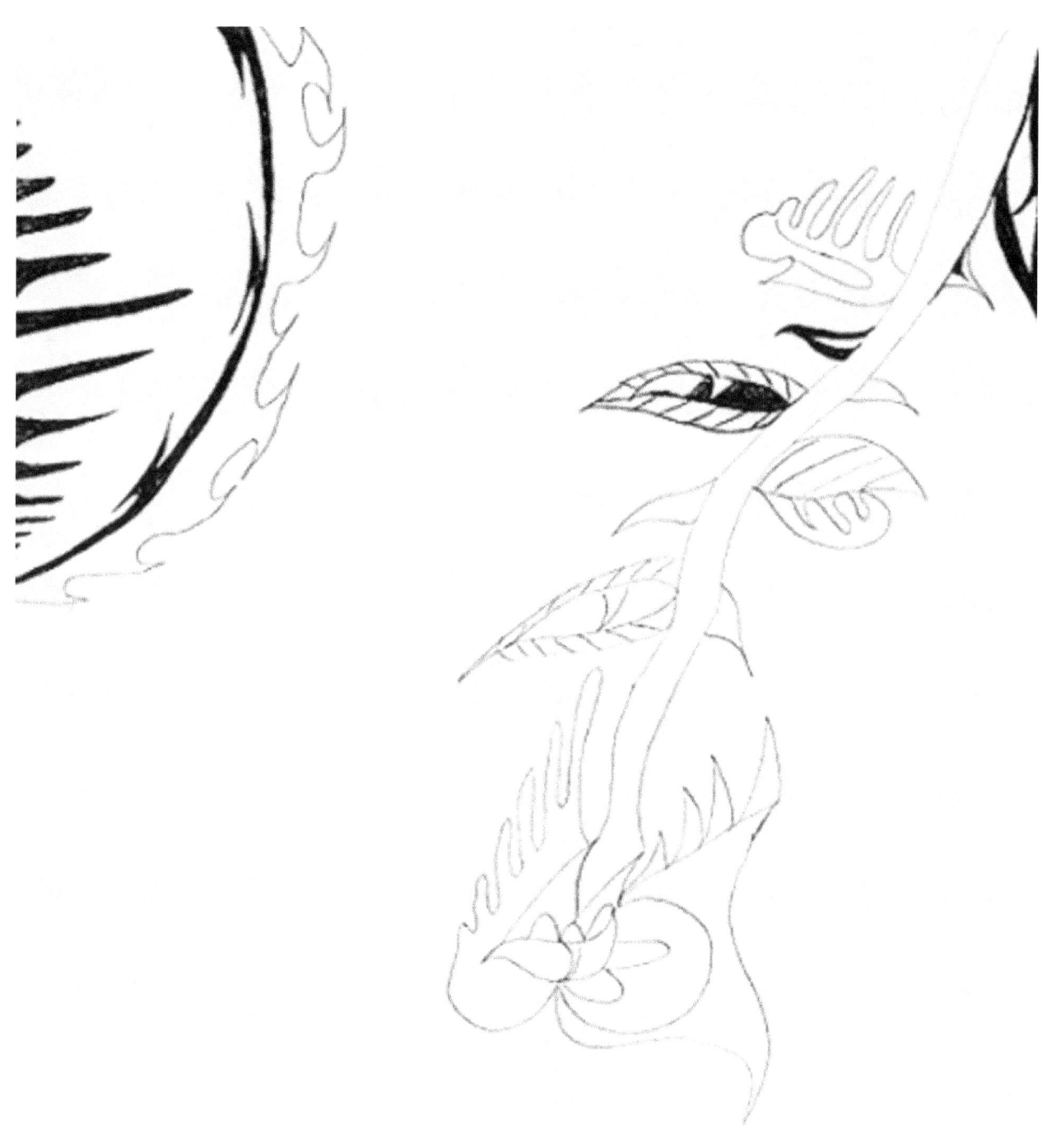

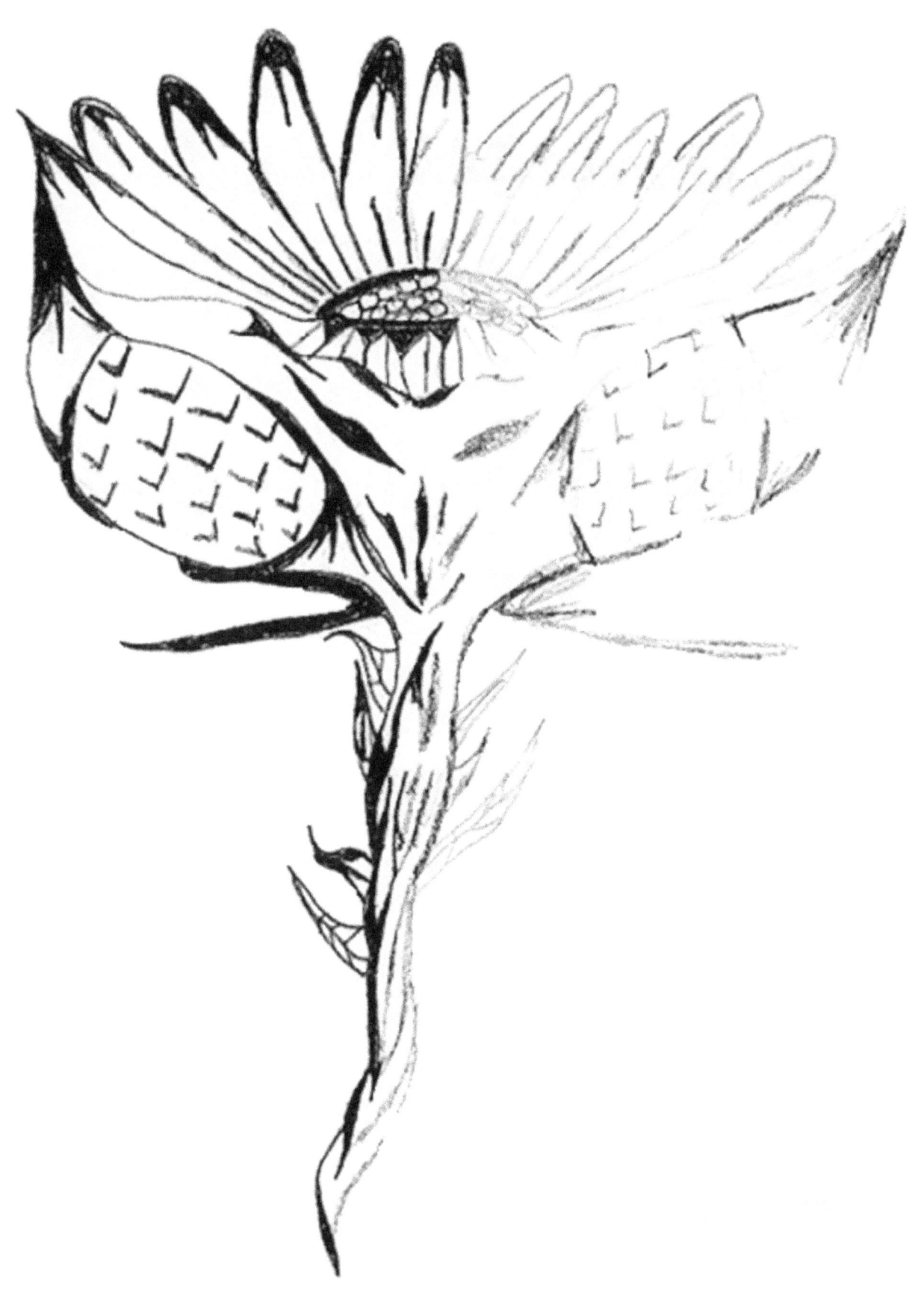

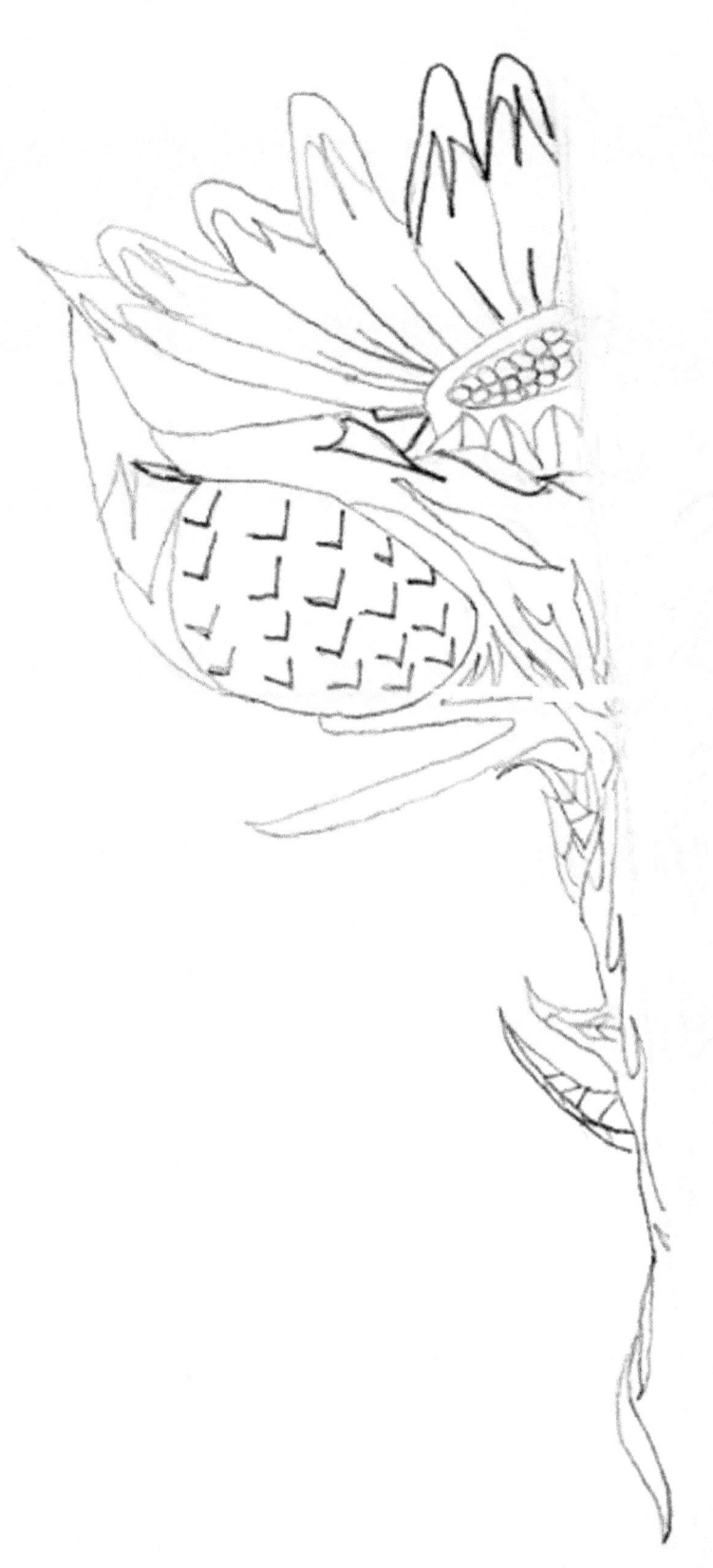

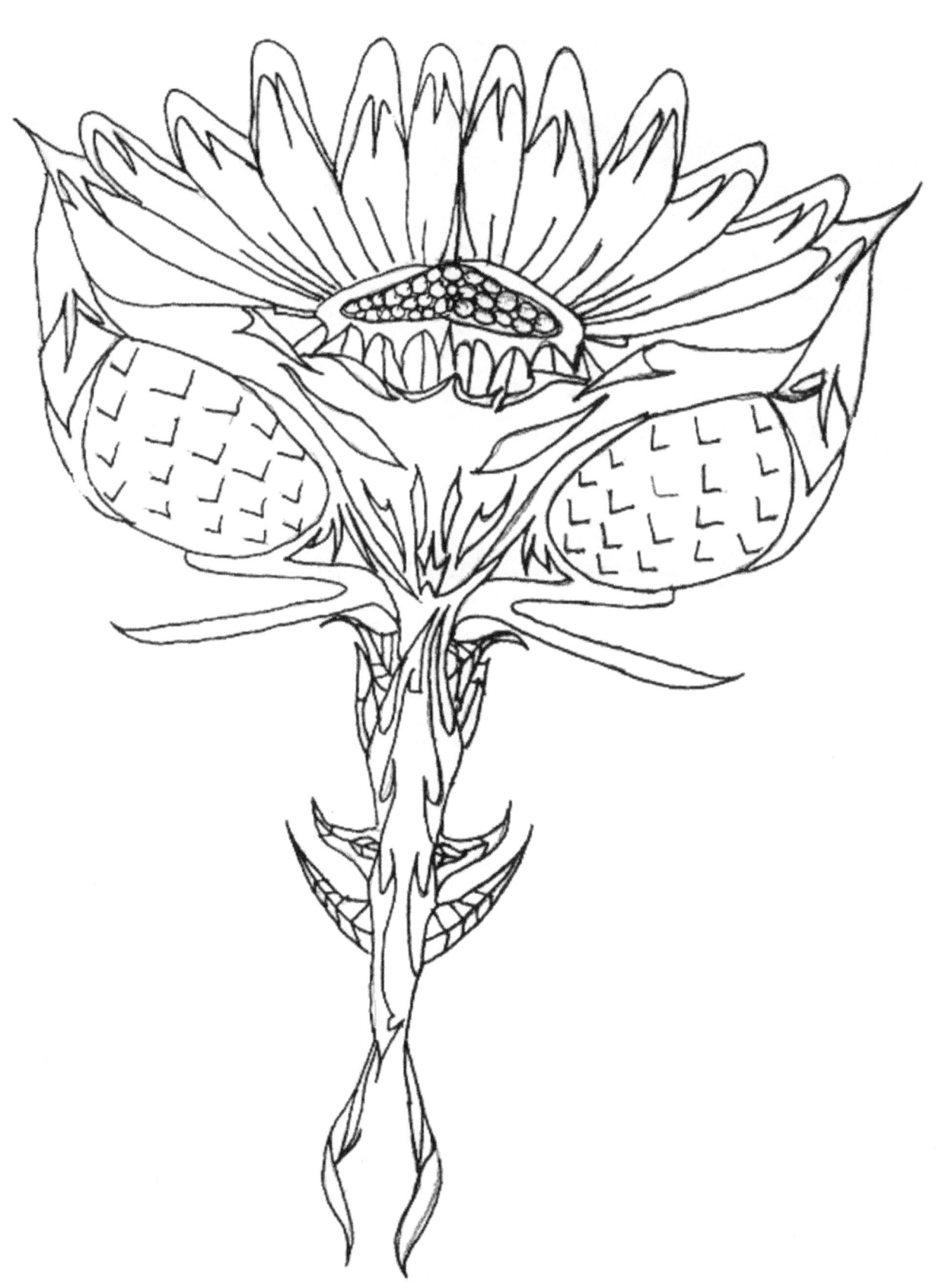

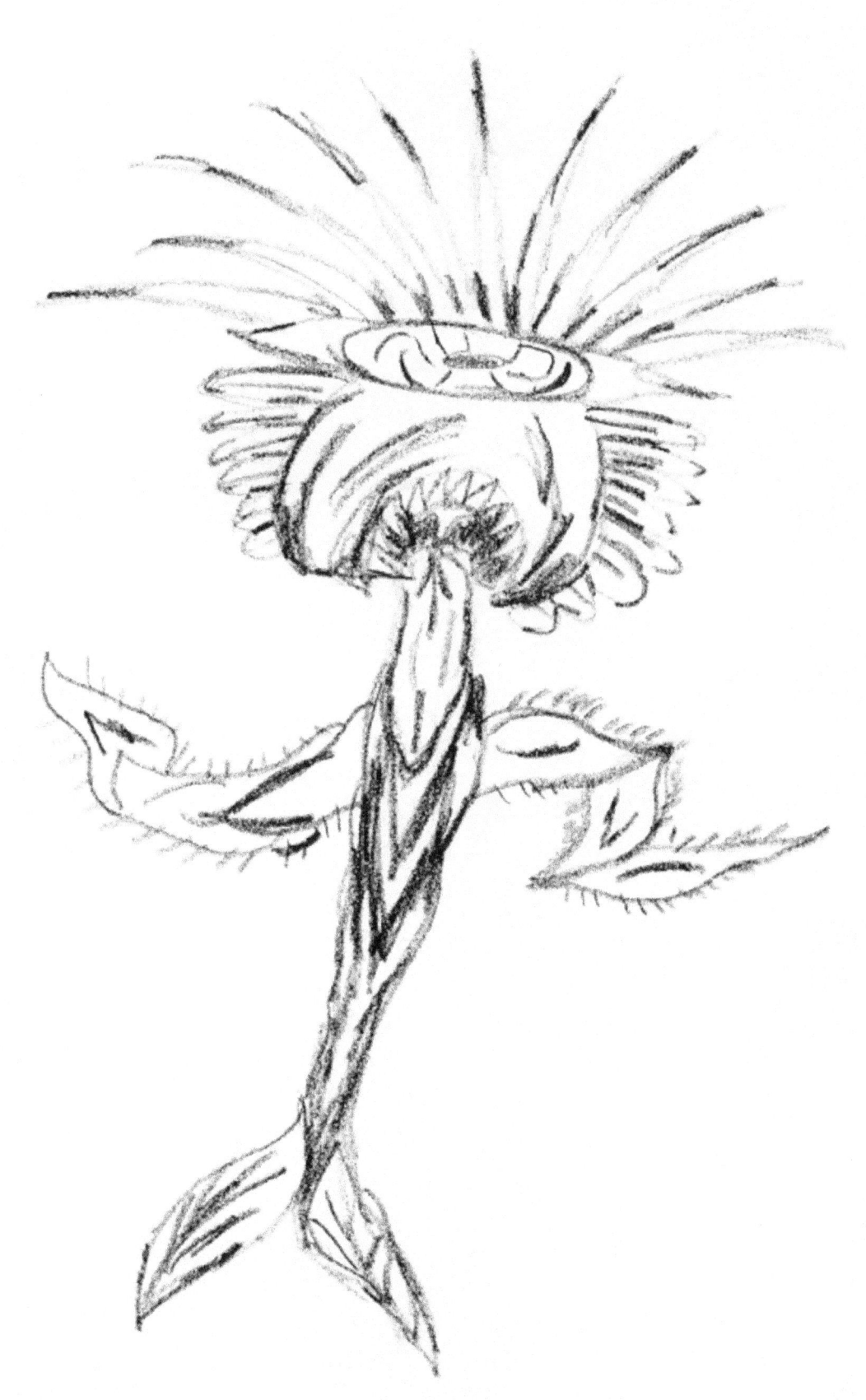

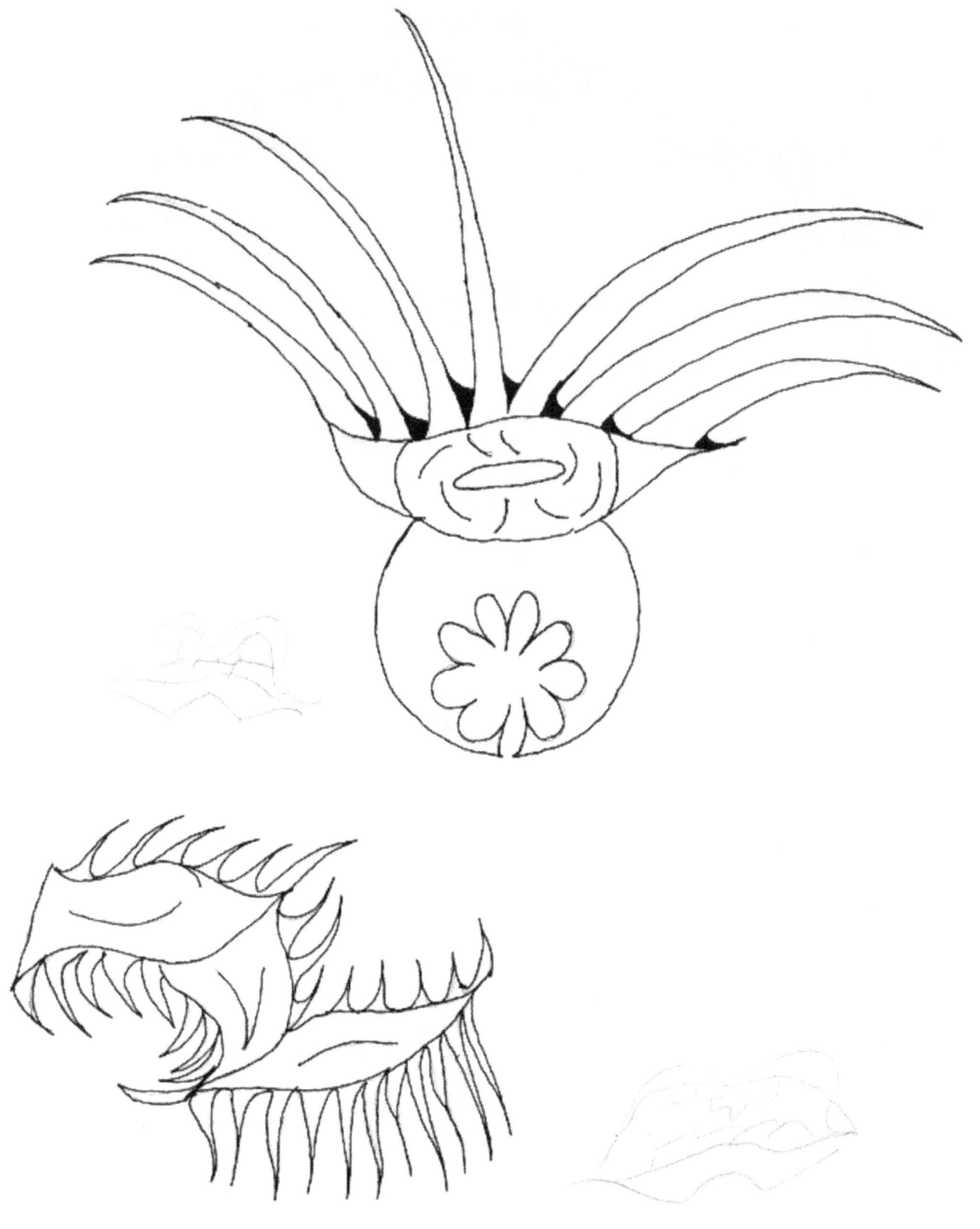

ABOUT THE ARTIST

Drew Calahan is a Congressional Award winning artist that resides in rural Missouri. He makes no claim of being a great artist or writer; just a passionate geek whom loves anime, 80s cartoons, and comics…and of course art and writing. His leisure time is spent split between his passions, his two boys and their pets (when the laser pen is working.)

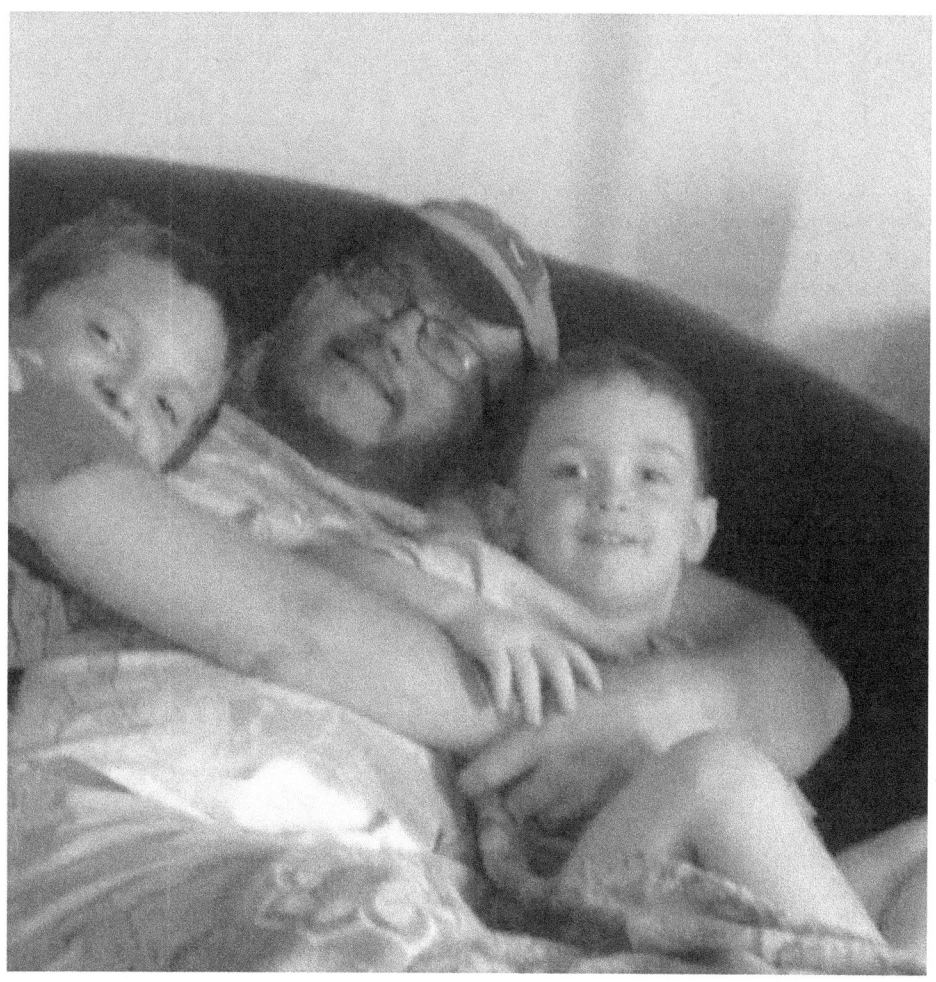

Other Works available or coming soon by H.A. "Drew" Calahan

The Writology series: A chronological journey of the writer's works from 5th grade through collegiate and post collegiate works. Rich with author commentary. The collection provides an inside view to the author's mind. Each volume comes with an appendix of suggested writing exercises based on either the original assignments that led to some the written creations or the creations themselves.

Volume 1: Bashful-less Beginnings
Volume 2: FreshMarks
Volume 3: SophStrokes
Volume 4: The Return
Volume 5: The Keystone Diary
Volume 6: FinalMarks
Volume 7: PostScript I
Volume 8: The Brown Mackie Papers
Volume 9: PostScript II
Volume 10: The Black Book

The Artology series is a visual journey of the artist's works. Similar to Writology, works range from early grade school to collegiate and post collegiate efforts. However, the work is grouped according to subject matter. The artist does provide some commentary on selected works. The commentary offers the viewer/reader an inside view to the artist's interpretation or inspirations behind the works.

Volume 1: 1st Steps
Volume 2: LifeScapes and LandStills
Volume 3: Mock Civil War Sketchbook
Volume 4: Colorado Sketchbook
Volume 5: Mock Court Trial Sketchbook
Volume 6: Not So Portait-tific
Volume 7: Creature Feature
Volume 8: Spoof Party!
Volume 9: The Abstract Clause I: Hands Alive
Volume 10: The Abstract Clause II: Celestial Addiction
Volume 11: The Abstract Clause III: About Face
Volume 12: Superhero Silo
Volume 13: The Meramec Years
Volume 14: Multiplicity
Volume 15: Cover Me Colors Crazy
Artology: The Coloring Book (A Designs by Drew Collection)

*Please note that for either the Writology or Artology series, some volumes may be multi-released within a single published collection. Works can be found on **www.lulu.com** and **www.createspace.com** Search according to series, title, **"H.A. Calahan"** or **geekyinker**. Additional works also on **www.redbubble.com/people/geekyinker** Find me on Facebook at **www.facebook.com/DesignsByDrewCalahan** for artist/writer news, updates, product launches, contests, give-a-ways and more!

Additional forthcoming works planned by H.A. Calahan include several children's books and a novel series.

Please send fan or professional correspondences to:
drew.5gstudios@gmail.com

H.A. Calahan is not responsible for printing or shipping/handling issues.